Laravel 12 Cookbook

Second Edition

Build, secure, and scale your apps with solutions across authentication, routing, security, media, APIs, queues, scheduling and automation

Sanya Voltra

Published by: GitforGits

www.gitforgits.com

Printed in India

First Printing: April 2026

ISBN: 978-93-49174-82-5

Cover Design by: Kitten Publishing

Disclaimer:

This book, including all its text, diagrams, and illustrations, is an original work developed for educational and informational purposes. The content is not affiliated with, endorsed by, or sponsored by or any other company, brand, or entity referenced within. All brand names, product names, and trademarks mentioned are the property of their respective owners and are used in a descriptive, educational context only. Every effort has been made to ensure that no copyrighted or trademarked material has been copied or misused in this book. All diagrams and illustrations that are not original have been used with proper attribution and credit to their respective sources.

If you believe that any content in this book infringes upon your copyright or trademark, please contact us immediately at support@gitforgits.com. Upon notification, corrective action will be taken promptly.

Prologue

At some point, every developer has that lightbulb moment when a framework feels less like a bunch of rules and more like a real language. It's a language you think in, not just write in. For me, that moment came with Laravel. In my years of experience, I've worked on PHP projects that were smart but not very stable, and they were quick to build but slow to trust. Then I found Laravel, and something shifted. The code started talking. The routes were all set. The middleware just clicked into place, like the last piece of a lock. And Eloquent, which is elegant, fluid and almost poetic, made the database feel less like a constraint and more like a collaborator.

That feeling never left me. But frameworks grow. And teams grow. The number of applications is growing. And what felt like enough at first is starting to show its true colours. A notification system that works for ten users can't handle ten thousand. If a migration goes smoothly in development, but fails silently in production, we need to know. A task that was scheduled and no one thought twice about starts overlapping itself at 2 a.m. and messing up the output, which no one finds out about until the morning. This book came about because of those edges. It's not about being in the comfortable middle where things are working fine, but more about being out of that zone where they stop working and you need to know exactly the reason why and what to do next.

I'd say Laravel 12 is a pretty mature and confident framework. It's ditched old habits, tweaked its bootstrap configuration, given its scheduler a modern makeover, and adopted a filesystem-first approach to media management. PHP 8.5 has some great new features that make our code cleaner and clearer. So, when you put these two together, you've basically got the best version of the Laravel ecosystem there's ever been. And that's the perfect base for those serious, production-grade apps that users can really count on. All the recipes in this book were created to solve a real problem. The RBAC middleware is there to protect admin routes. The job chain that processes reports without blocking HTTP responses. The Intervention Image pipeline is great for resizing a thousand product photos without putting a strain on the server. The Prunable trait is pretty handy because it removes stale records every night while the team is asleep. These aren't academic exercises. They're the solutions I went for when the app needed them, and I've refined them over and over again based on feedback from production and users, turning them into patterns I'm proud to pass on.

I wrote this book for developers who already know Laravel but want to know it better. Who's the one who's got your back on the easy days and is there for you on the tough ones? I believe that great backend architecture isn't about complexity, it's about clarity, reliability and the kind of quiet confidence that comes from knowing your system will hold. We're going to build that system together, one recipe at a time.

Welcome to the second edition!

Content

Preface

There's nothing like this out there. It's an absolute recipe-based book for PHP developers covering practical, battle-tested solutions for building, securing and maintaining production-grade Laravel 12 applications on Linux. It's all broken down into a bunch of focused recipes that actually tackle some of the real-world backend challenges you might face. From scratch, you'll get to configure a secure PHP 8.5 and Laravel 12 environment, design expressive Eloquent models with complex relationships, and enforce layered authentication and role-based access control using Breeze, Socialite, and Fortify. And you'll get to grips with database migrations, model factories, query optimisation and Eloquent scopes, too. That way, you'll be able to keep your data layer clean and performant.

There's loads of interesting stuff on robust data validation and centralised exception handling. I'll show you to build multi-channel notification systems, integrate real-time broadcasting with Pusher and Laravel Echo, and offload heavy work to queued jobs with retry strategies, chaining, and batching. We'll go through file storage, media management, image processing with Intervention Image v3, and secure S3 integration in detail, as well as temporary signed URL generation and a reusable media registry. And the last few chapters are all about automation and reliability, like scheduling tasks using routes/console.php, running automated database backups with Spatie Laravel Backup, getting rid of stale data with the Prunable trait, and keeping an eye on your app's health with Telescope and Pulse.

All the recipes use the only one and the same project, so you get a consistent, cumulative set of code, rather than a bunch of random examples that you can't even connect.

In this book you will learn to:

- Make a production-ready Laravel 12 environment on Linux from scratch.
- Create eloquent relationships and optimize queries using eager loading and scopes.
- Implement layered authentication with Breeze, Socialite, Fortify, and RBAC middleware.
- Run server-side validation with custom closure rules and tailored error messages.
- Centralize exception handling using Laravel 12's bootstrap-first withExceptions callback.
- Dispatch, chain, and batch background jobs with robust retry and failure handling.
- Deliver real-time notifications via database, email, SMS, and WebSocket broadcasting.
- Process, resize, and store media securely using Intervention Image v3 and AWS S3.
- Automate recurring maintenance tasks using routes/console.php and Linux cron.
- Monitor application health and prune stale data through Pulse, Telescope, and Prunable models.

GitforGits

Prerequisites

This book is a practical, problem-solving recipe-based book, built for PHP developers who want to build, secure and maintain production-grade Laravel 12 applications on Linux. All you need is some prior experience in using Laravel of any past versions.

Codes Usage

Are you in need of some helpful code examples to assist you in your programming and documentation? Look no further! Our book offers a wealth of supplemental material, including code examples and exercises.

Not only is this book here to aid you in getting your job done, but you have our permission to use the example code in your programs and documentation. However, please note that if you are reproducing a significant portion of the code, we do require you to contact us for permission.

But don't worry, using several chunks of code from this book in your program or answering a question by citing our book and quoting example code does not require permission. But if you do choose to give credit, an attribution typically includes the title, author, publisher, and ISBN. For example, " Laravel 12 Cookbook, Second Edition by Sanya Voltra".

If you are unsure whether your intended use of the code examples falls under fair use or the permissions outlined above, please do not hesitate to reach out to us at support@gitforgits.com.

We are happy to assist and clarify any concerns.

Acknowledgement

I owe a tremendous debt of gratitude to GitforGits, for their unflagging enthusiasm and wise counsel throughout the entire process of writing this book. Their knowledge and careful editing helped make sure the piece was useful for people of all reading levels and comprehension skills. In addition, I'd like to thank everyone involved in the publishing process for their efforts in making this book a reality. Their efforts, from copyediting to advertising, made the project what it is today.

Finally, I'd like to express my gratitude to everyone who has shown me unconditional love and encouragement throughout my life. Their support was crucial to the completion of this book. I appreciate your help with this endeavour and your continued interest in my career.

Chapter 1
Setting up PHP 8.5 and Laravel 12

Overview

In this chapter, we will walk through setting up a Linux-based development environment specifically for Laravel 12. We will begin by updating our Linux system and installing PHP 8.5 along with its required extensions. Then, we will set up Composer to manage our dependencies and install Laravel 12, which will keep our project framework well organized. We will also learn how to configure essential environment variables and generate an application key for security purposes. We will also explore the importance of Laravel's directory layout and how to manage file permissions to keep things secure and running smoothly.

Next, we will assemble a solid set of tools for development, including PhpStorm, Laravel Debugbar, and Telescope, which will make our workflow and debugging process far more effective. Finally, we will set up Git version control, establish commit conventions, and configure remote repositories to enable seamless collaboration with the team. Every skill we build in this chapter will carry us into the more advanced territory ahead with confidence.

Recipe 1: Installing PHP 8.5 and Laravel 12 using Composer

You work in a lively office where a new Linux server was just delivered to our team. The system is completely barebones, with no PHP, Composer, or Laravel installed, and we are all set to dive in and get everything up and running. Today, we are laying the groundwork for an exciting project by installing PHP 8.5 as the base for Laravel 12. We will use Composer as our primary dependency manager to fetch Laravel, configure essential environment variables, and verify that everything is working. This live scenario is set up so that each step builds on the last, getting us ready for a smooth transition into more advanced development tasks.

Installing PHP 8.5

Before diving into new installations, we will first update our Linux server to ensure that every package is current. We now run this update command:

```
sudo apt update && sudo apt upgrade -y
```

The above command synchronizes our package listings with the latest repository data and upgrades any pre-installed packages. This step provides us with a fresh system that has no potential conflicts or errors in later installations. It is always a good practice to begin any server setup by confirming that the base system is fully up to date, since outdated packages can introduce subtle incompatibilities that are difficult to diagnose later on.

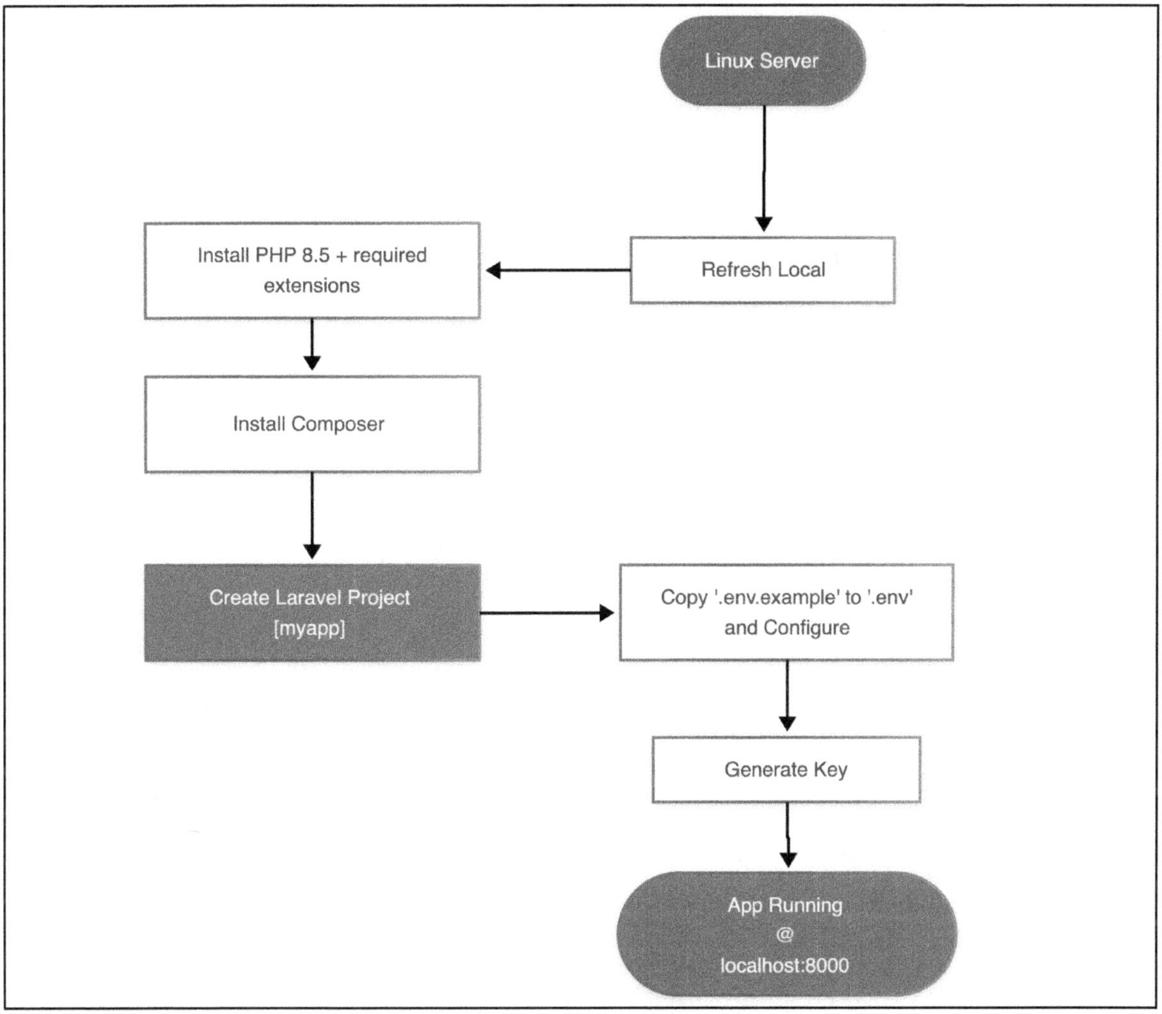

Fig 1.1: Laravel 12 Installation Workflow

Our Laravel 12 framework relies on PHP 8.5, so the next step is installing this version along with a set of critical extensions. These extensions will empower our application by handling string operations, XML parsing, network communications, and file compression. Here, we install PHP 8.5 and its extensions:

```
sudo apt install php8.5 php8.5-common php8.5-cli php8.5-mbstring
php8.5-xml php8.5-curl php8.5-zip -y
```

After the installation completes, we can try to make sure everything is in place by checking the PHP version. So here, we will try checking the installed version:

```
php -v
```

The terminal will display details about the installed PHP version. The output will look similar to this:

```
pravindhandre — -zsh — 80×24

pravindhandre@Pravins-MacBook-Air ~ % php -v
PHP 8.5.6 (cli) (built: May  5 2026 21:19:36) (NTS)
Copyright (c) The PHP Group
Built by Homebrew
Zend Engine v4.5.6, Copyright (c) Zend Technologies
    with Zend OPcache v8.5.6, Copyright (c), by Zend Technologies
pravindhandre@Pravins-MacBook-Air ~ %
```

Fig 1.2: PHP Version Check

This output confirms that PHP 8.5 is correctly installed and ready to support our Laravel 12 project on this Linux server.

Installing Composer

Now that PHP is installed, it is time to set up Composer, the go-to tool for managing PHP dependencies. It automatically handles the libraries needed for our project, saving us time and reducing manual errors. With Composer, we can effortlessly download and manage updates to Laravel and all its required components. Without this tool, managing dependencies across a growing Laravel application would be a tedious and error-prone process.

Next, we download the Composer installer script directly to our current directory:

```
curl -sS https://getcomposer.org/installer -o composer-setup.php
```

This will download the Composer installer script to our current directory. Once the download is complete, we will want to verify the integrity of the installer by comparing its hash to the one provided on Composer's official website. After ensuring the script is safe, we will then run the installer with PHP:

```
php composer-setup.php --install-dir=/usr/local/bin --filename=composer
```

This command places Composer in the **`/usr/local/bin`** directory, allowing us to invoke it from anywhere on the system. Once Composer is installed, we can perform a clean-up by removing the installer file. At this point, we remove it:

```
rm composer-setup.php
```

Finally, we will confirm that Composer is ready for action. We can now run:

```
composer --version
```

It will display the installed Composer version:

```
pravindhandre — -zsh — 80×24

pravindhandre@Pravins-MacBook-Air ~ % composer --version
Composer version 2.9.7 2026-04-14 13:31:52
PHP version 8.5.6 (/opt/homebrew/Cellar/php/8.5.6/bin/php)
Run the "diagnose" command to get more detailed diagnostics output.
pravindhandre@Pravins-MacBook-Air ~ %
```

Fig 1.3: Composer Version

Installing Laravel 12

With PHP and Composer successfully installed, we will now proceed to install Laravel 12. To do this, we will create a new project directory named **`myapp`** and run this Composer command:

```
composer create-project --prefer-dist laravel/laravel myapp "12.*"
```

This instructs Composer to fetch Laravel version 12 along with all its dependencies. The command not only downloads the required packages but also organizes our project directory with well-defined folders like **`app`**, **`config`**, **`database`**, and **`resources`**. Each of these folders serves a specific purpose within the Laravel architecture, and we will encounter them frequently as we build out our application in subsequent chapters.

```
pravindhandre — -zsh — 80×24
pravindhandre@Pravins-MacBook-Air ~ % composer create-project --prefer-dist laravel/laravel myapp "12.*"
Creating a "laravel/laravel" project at "./myapp"
  - Installing laravel/laravel (v12.20.0): Extracting archive
Created project in /Users/pravindhandre/myapp
  - Installing laravel/framework (v12.58.0): Extracting archive
  - Installing laravel/tinker (v2.11.1): Extracting archive
  - Installing nunomaduro/collision (v8.9.4): Extracting archive
  - Installing symfony/http-kernel (v7.4.10): Extracting archive
    ... (81 packages installed)
Generating optimized autoload files
> Illuminate\Foundation\ComposerScripts::postAutoloadDump
> @php artisan package:discover --ansi
 INFO  Discovering packages.
  laravel/pail ........................................................ DONE
  laravel/sail ........................................................ DONE
  laravel/tinker ...................................................... DONE
  nesbot/carbon ....................................................... DONE
  nunomaduro/collision ................................................ DONE
  nunomaduro/termwind ................................................. DONE
81 packages you are using are looking for funding.
Use the `composer fund` command to find out more!
> @php artisan key:generate --ansi
 INFO  Application key set successfully.
No security vulnerability advisories found.
pravindhandre@Pravins-MacBook-Air ~ %
```

Fig 1.4: Creating Laravel Project

After this, we will move into our new project directory through::

```
cd myapp
```

At this point, we will notice that Laravel's standard structure is already in place. This is our playground for developing everything from basic routes to complex business logic, and every chapter in this book will build upon this same **myapp** project.

Configuring Environment Variables

Setting up Environment file

The Laravel framework comes with a sample environment configuration file named **.env.example**. We need to customize this file to match our specific Linux setup.

So here, we will then copy the example to create a usable **.env** file:

```
cp .env.example .env
```

Our new **.env** file will store critical settings like database credentials, mail configurations, and the application key. This separation of configuration from the codebase is essential as we begin to add more functionality and eventually move into production.

Generating Application Key

A unique application key secures our encrypted data and user sessions. From here, we generate this key:

```
php artisan key:generate
```

It automatically updates the **.env** file with a newly generated key. It acts as a safeguard against a range of vulnerabilities, and the output will confirm that the key has been set.

```
myapp — -zsh — 80×24

pravindhandre@Pravins-MacBook-Air ~ % cd myapp
pravindhandre@Pravins-MacBook-Air myapp % php artisan key:generate
 INFO  Application key set successfully.
pravindhandre@Pravins-MacBook-Air myapp %
```

Fig 1.5: Application Key Generated

Without this key, Laravel will refuse to serve requests, making this step non-negotiable before we proceed any further.

Verifying Laravel Setup

To ensure that everything is running smoothly, we will now start the built-in Laravel development server using Artisan. We then launch it:

```
php artisan serve
```

The terminal will display the local server address as shown below:

```
INFO  Server running on [http://127.0.0.1:8000].


  Press Ctrl+C to stop the server
```

After this, we can open a web browser and navigate to **http://127.0.0.1:8000**.

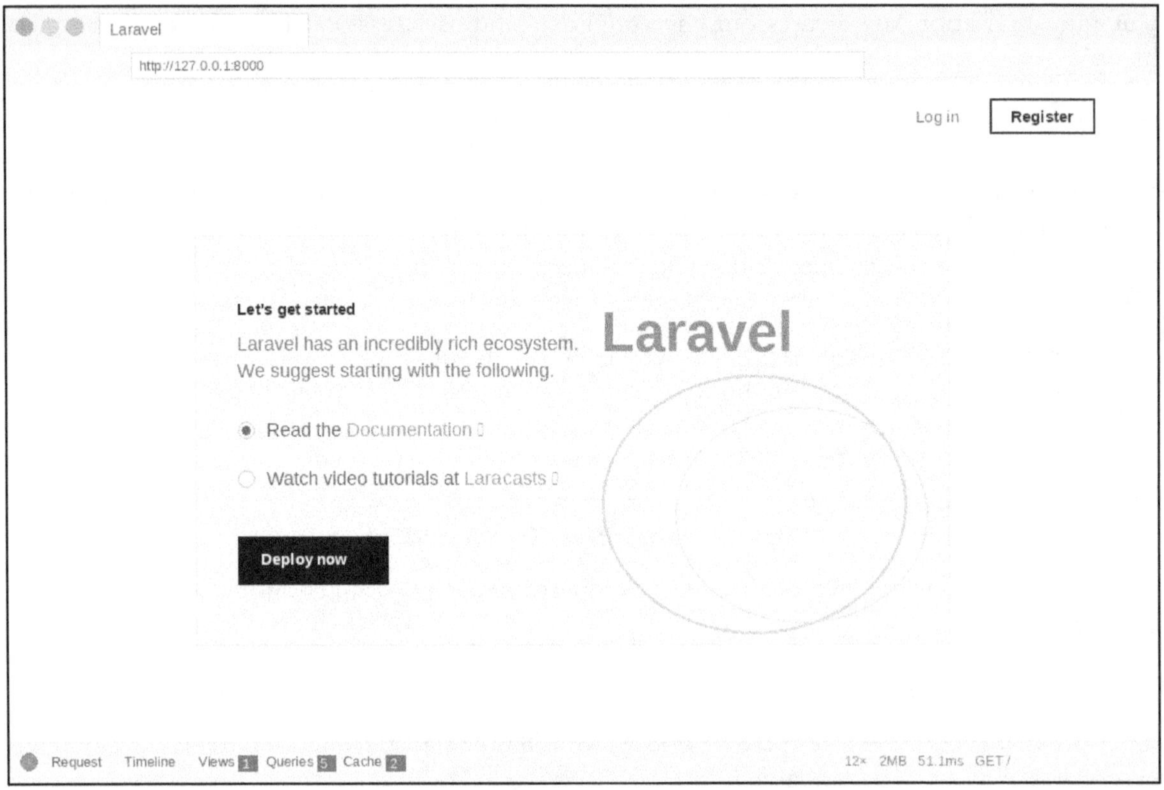

Fig 1.6: Laravel Welcome Page on Browser

We should see Laravel's welcome page, which is our first confirmation that the installation was successful and that our Linux server is now fully configured for Laravel 12 development.

Recipe 2: Configuring Linux File Permissions and Directory Structure

Now that we have PHP, Composer, and Laravel 12 set up on our Linux machine as covered in the previous recipe, it is time to move on. We can think of having a basic system configured for Laravel, and it is starting to receive data and user interactions. In our busy office, we will work on this project by tweaking its structure and security through hands-on work with the Linux file system. We will confidently navigate the Laravel directory structure and learn essential Linux commands, including listing directories, managing ownership, and modifying file permissions. Once we get the hang of these concepts, we will be well equipped to keep our project running smoothly and reliably.

Revisiting Laravel Project Structure

Before diving into permissions, let us refresh our understanding of the directory structure we created in the first recipe. First, we will navigate to our project folder. We now run:

```
cd myapp
```

Now, we will list the contents of the directory to get a clear picture of what Laravel has generated for us:

```
ls -l
```

We will see a well-organized layout with folders such as **`app`**, **`bootstrap`**, **`config`**, **`database`**, **`public`**, **`resources`**, **`storage`**, and **`vendor`**.

```
myapp — -zsh — 80×24

pravindhandre@Pravins-MacBook-Air myapp % ls -l
total 656
drwxr-xr-x   5 pravindhandre  staff     160 14 Mar 22:24 app
-rwxr-xr-x   1 pravindhandre  staff     425 14 Mar 22:24 artisan
drwxr-xr-x   5 pravindhandre  staff     160 14 Mar 22:24 bootstrap
-rw-r--r--   1 pravindhandre  staff    2849 14 Mar 22:24 composer.json
-rw-r--r--   1 pravindhandre  staff  309792  9 May 10:42 composer.lock
drwxr-xr-x  12 pravindhandre  staff     384 14 Mar 22:24 config
drwxr-xr-x   7 pravindhandre  staff     224  9 May 10:42 database
-rw-r--r--   1 pravindhandre  staff     414 14 Mar 22:24 package.json
-rw-r--r--   1 pravindhandre  staff    1322 14 Mar 22:24 phpunit.xml
drwxr-xr-x   6 pravindhandre  staff     192 14 Mar 22:24 public
-rw-r--r--   1 pravindhandre  staff    3911 14 Mar 22:24 README.md
drwxr-xr-x   5 pravindhandre  staff     160 14 Mar 22:24 resources
drwxr-xr-x   4 pravindhandre  staff     128 14 Mar 22:24 routes
drwxr-xr-x   5 pravindhandre  staff     160 14 Mar 22:24 storage
drwxr-xr-x   5 pravindhandre  staff     160 14 Mar 22:24 tests
drwxr-xr-x  40 pravindhandre  staff    1280  9 May 10:42 vendor
-rw-r--r--   1 pravindhandre  staff     436 14 Mar 22:24 vite.config.js
pravindhandre@Pravins-MacBook-Air myapp %
```

Fig 1.7: Project Root Listing

Each folder plays a key role in the application's operation. For instance, the **`storage`** directory is where Laravel writes logs, caches, and files, while **`bootstrap/cache`** holds crucial cache files that improve performance. Recognizing these components is essential since, as our project evolves, these files and directories become critical for both functionality and security.

Checking Default Permissions

The file permissions on our Linux server dictate who can read, write, or execute our project files. Here, we inspect the permissions currently in place:

```
ls -l
```

The output will show us details like **drwxr-xr-x** for each directory. In this notation, we will notice three sets of permissions representing the file owner, the group, and others. For Laravel to operate correctly, certain directories such as **storage** and **bootstrap/cache** require write permissions for the web server. Without these permissions, Laravel will be unable to write logs, cache views, or store uploaded files.

Configuring Directory Permissions

Now, we will secure our Laravel project by ensuring that the web server can appropriately write to critical directories while maintaining a secure overall structure. In our Linux environment, the web server commonly runs under a specific user account such as **www-data**. This means that **storage** and **bootstrap/cache** must be owned by or accessible to this user for proper operation. Neglecting this step is one of the most common causes of permission-related errors in fresh Laravel installations.

Changing Ownership

To assign the correct owner and group recursively for the **storage** and **bootstrap/cache** directories, we now run:

```
sudo chown -R www-data:www-data storage bootstrap/cache
```

It assigns **www-data** as both the owner and group for these directories, ensuring that files created by Laravel will carry the correct access rights for the web server. This step is critical for both security and functionality, as improper ownership can lead to application errors that are sometimes difficult to trace back to their root cause.

Modifying Permissions

Next, we will update the directory permissions so that the owner and group have full read, write, and execute permissions, while others can read and execute only. We now apply this command:

```
sudo chmod -R 775 storage bootstrap/cache
```

The permission code **775** guarantees that we, as part of the group, and the web server can modify files in these directories. This is necessary for writing logs, caching data, and handling file uploads. It also blocks unauthorized modifications from other users on the system, striking the right balance between openness and security.

To verify that these changes have been applied correctly, we will then inspect the directory details. At this point, we run these two commands:

```
ls -l storage
```

```
ls -l bootstrap/cache
```

We should see permissions resembling **drwxrwxr-x** for these directories. This output confirms that our adjustments are in place, and both we and the web server can manage the files needed for optimal Laravel performance.

Laravel's Access to File System

It is important to be well versed in how Laravel leverages these directories throughout the lifecycle of our project. The **storage** directory is not merely a random folder; it is the central hub for dynamic content. It stores application logs in **storage/logs**, caches compiled views and configuration files in **storage/framework**, and even temporarily holds uploaded files. If we ever encounter issues related to caching or log generation, revisiting these permissions is often the very first troubleshooting step we should take.

Similarly, the **bootstrap/cache** directory is crucial during the application bootstrapping process. Laravel compiles configuration and route files into this directory to reduce overhead during request handling. If the web server cannot write to this directory because of strict permissions, we could face runtime errors or slower performance that degrades the user experience in ways that are hard to diagnose without understanding the underlying file system structure.

Practical Linux Commands

As we continue working on our Laravel application, we will rely on a handful of Linux commands regularly. To check the file structure and permissions, we use **ls -l** to list files and directories in detail. To set the correct ownership for directories, we use **chown**, ensuring our web server and development tools have the right access. To grant or restrict access according to our project's needs, we apply **chmod**. And for a clearer visual overview of our project's structure, we can install the **tree** command. We can now install it:

```
sudo apt install tree
```

After installation, we now visualize our project directory structure up to two levels deep:

```
tree -L 2
```

Once we get the hang of these Linux commands, we will be able to troubleshoot and maintain our Laravel project more effectively as new challenges arise. Every new command and configuration builds naturally on what we have already mastered, equipping us with practical skills that will be essential at every subsequent phase of our development work.

Recipe 3: Configuring Linux Tools for Laravel

Now that we have successfully installed Laravel 12 and worked through its file structure and permissions on our Linux system, it is time to take things up a notch by setting up a suite of development tools that will streamline our daily workflow. Just picture our team at the start of a new project meeting, where everyone is eager to see how a solid development environment can boost overall productivity. In our development station, we will set up essential tools including PhpStorm for a feature-rich IDE, Laravel Debugbar for real-time debugging, and Laravel Telescope for advanced monitoring. These tools will serve us well when we are ready to tackle more demanding topics like debugging and performance analysis.

Setting up PhpStorm

PhpStorm is a powerful IDE that provides intelligent code assistance and debugging features, making it well suited for Laravel development. There are a few ways to install PhpStorm on Linux, but using Snap simplifies the process considerably. From here, we execute this command:

```
sudo snap install phpstorm --classic
```

This will install PhpStorm with classic confinement, ensuring that all the necessary system privileges are granted. Once installed, we can launch PhpStorm from our application menu or by typing this command in the terminal:

```
phpstorm
```

After starting PhpStorm, we are prompted to configure initial settings like themes, keymaps, and plugins. At this point, we will want to install two recommended plugins, the Laravel Plugin for Blade support and route navigation, and PHP Intelephense for code intelligence. We can add these plugins via File > Settings > Plugins, then search for each by name. After installing them, we will restart PhpStorm to activate the enhancements, and our IDE will become a powerful extension of our Linux development environment.

Installing Laravel Debugbar

The Laravel Debugbar is an indispensable tool during development. It provides a real-time overview of the application's internal processes, such as route handling, database queries, and log messages. This insight is especially useful as we continue to refine our application and track down performance bottlenecks that might otherwise go unnoticed during development.

We then integrate Debugbar into our project by navigating to the project directory and running this command:

```
composer require barryvdh/laravel-debugbar --dev
```

This then installs the Debugbar package as a development dependency. Once the package is installed, Laravel automatically registers the Debugbar service provider through its package auto-discovery feature.

```
myapp — -zsh — 80×24

pravindhandre@Pravins-MacBook-Air myapp % composer require barryvdh/laravel-debugbar --dev
Generating optimized autoload files
> Illuminate\Foundation\ComposerScripts::postAutoloadDump
> @php artisan package:discover --ansi
 INFO  Discovering packages.
  barryvdh/laravel-debugbar ........................................ DONE
  laravel/pail .................................................... DONE
  laravel/sail .................................................... DONE
  laravel/tinker .................................................. DONE
  nesbot/carbon ................................................... DONE
  nunomaduro/collision ............................................ DONE
  nunomaduro/termwind ............................................. DONE
83 packages you are using are looking for funding.
No security vulnerability advisories found.
Using version ^4.2 for barryvdh/laravel-debugbar
pravindhandre@Pravins-MacBook-Air myapp %
```

Fig 1.8: Debugbar Installed

We may check our **config/app.php** file if we want to confirm the provider is loaded, though this typically happens without any manual intervention.

Next, after installation, we will start our project server. We now run:

```
php artisan serve
```

Now we can browse to **http://127.0.0.1:8000**. We should see a new Debugbar panel rendered at the bottom of our screen. This panel shows detailed insights about rendered views, executed queries, and processed middleware, giving us a live window into everything our application is doing on each request.

Setting up Laravel Telescope

The Laravel Telescope offers an advanced debugging and monitoring dashboard that records and displays information about every request entering our application. This tool complements Debugbar by providing a persistent record of application activity, making it easier for us to fine-tune our Laravel system as **myapp** scales. Here, we install Telescope within our project directory:

```
composer require laravel/telescope --dev
```

The Telescope package is pulled in as a development-only dependency, keeping it out of production builds as shown below:

```
myapp — -zsh — 80×24

pravindhandre@Pravins-MacBook-Air myapp % composer require laravel/telescope --dev
Generating optimized autoload files
> Illuminate\Foundation\ComposerScripts::postAutoloadDump
> @php artisan package:discover --ansi
 INFO  Discovering packages.
  barryvdh/laravel-debugbar ................................. DONE
  laravel/pail .............................................. DONE
  laravel/sail .............................................. DONE
  laravel/sentinel .......................................... DONE
  laravel/telescope ......................................... DONE
  laravel/tinker ............................................ DONE
  nesbot/carbon ............................................. DONE
  nunomaduro/collision ...................................... DONE
  nunomaduro/termwind ....................................... DONE
83 packages you are using are looking for funding.
No security vulnerability advisories found.
Using version ^5.20 for laravel/telescope
pravindhandre@Pravins-MacBook-Air myapp %
```

Fig 1.9: Telescope Installed

Once installed, we will then publish the Telescope's configuration and assets. For this, we will run:

```
php artisan telescope:install
```

Once the package is installed, the artisan command publishes Telescope's views, assets, and configuration:

```
myapp — -zsh — 80×24

pravindhandre@Pravins-MacBook-Air myapp % php artisan telescope:install
 INFO  Telescope assets published successfully.
pravindhandre@Pravins-MacBook-Air myapp %
```

Fig 1.10: Telescope Scaffolded

After publishing the assets, we will complete the installation by running our migrations:

```
php artisan migrate
```

The above commands set up Telescope's database tables and its configuration settings. Once completed, we will start our Laravel server. For this, we will then run:

```
php artisan serve
```

After this, we can navigate to **http://127.0.0.1:8000/telescope**. There, we will see

Telescope's dashboard populated with live data from our application. The interface allows us to inspect recent requests, exceptions, logs, and queries. It gives us a thorough window into our application's internals that proves invaluable during complex debugging sessions.

Integrating Essential Linux-Based Tools

While Git will be set up in full in the next recipe, it is worth noting that it serves as our steadfast companion in managing code changes throughout the project. On Linux, we can always check the status of our repository using **`git status`**. For more advanced terminal management, multiplexers like **`tmux`** allow us to run multiple sessions in a single terminal window.

So here, we will then install **`tmux`**:

```
sudo apt install tmux -y
```

These tools let us split our terminal window and monitor several processes at once. They become a genuine asset as we juggle tasks like watching server logs, running debugging sessions, and making live code edits simultaneously.

Recipe 4: Integrating Git into Laravel

Now that we have a fully functional Laravel 12 project on our Linux machine, we will make sure that every team member can collaborate effectively. In the shared development environment of our office, we need to set up a solid version control system for **`myapp`**. Git is the industry standard for version control, and it lets us track changes, maintain commit history, and sync code across multiple developers.

In this recipe, we will walk through setting up a Git repository in **`myapp`**, establishing commit conventions, and configuring remote repositories, all using Linux terminal commands.

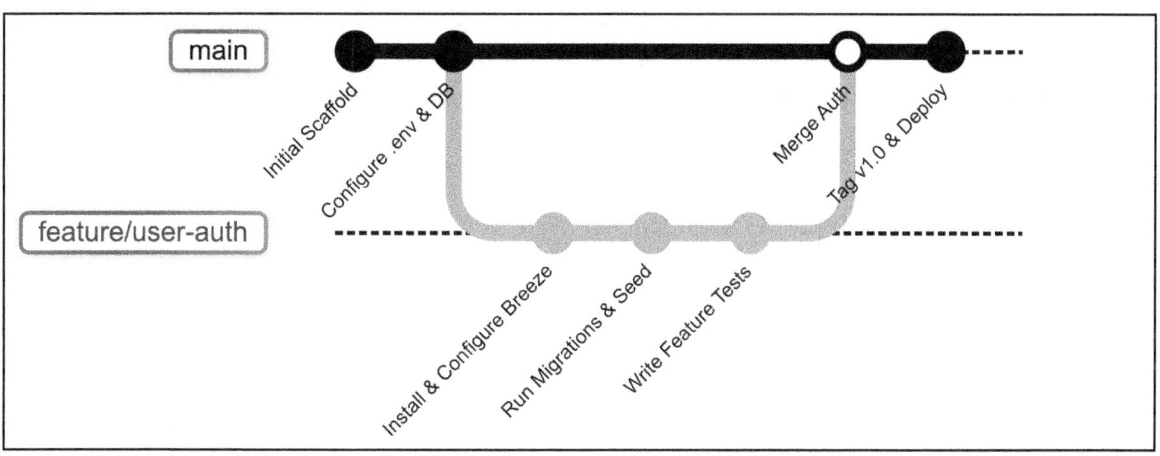

Fig 1.11: Version Control Workflow

The Git graph above illustrates a typical branching and merging cycle for a Laravel feature, from the initial scaffold commit through to a production merge:

Initializing Git Repository

First, we will navigate into **`myapp`** and we run:

```
cd myapp
```

At this point, we initialize Git:

```
git init
```

It sets up a new Git repository in our project folder, creating a hidden **`.git`** directory where Git will store all version history and configuration settings. From this point on, every change we make to **`myapp`** can be tracked, reviewed, and rolled back if needed.

```
myapp — -zsh — 80×24

pravindhandre@Pravins-MacBook-Air myapp % git init
Initialized empty Git repository in /Users/pravindhandre/myapp/.git/
pravindhandre@Pravins-MacBook-Air myapp %
```

Fig 1.12: Git Repository Initialized

Configuring Commit Conventions

Before adding files to our repository, it is important to tell Git which files or directories to exclude.

Creating .gitignore file

The Laravel comes with a default **`.gitignore`** file, but we should verify that it excludes sensitive and unnecessary files like cached data, logs, and environmental configuration. So here, we will open **`.gitignore`** file in the project root and ensure it contains entries similar to :

```
/vendor
/node_modules
/public/storage
/storage/*.key
.env
```

These entries help maintain a clean repository by avoiding the inclusion of large binaries and sensitive credentials that should never be shared across the team.

Adding files to Repository

Now, we will add the project files to the repository. We can now stage all current files:

```
git add .
```

This command stages all current files in our directory for the first commit. After staging, we will make our initial commit with a clear, descriptive message. From here, we commit:

```
git commit -m "Initial commit: Laravel 12 project setup with base configuration"
```

Establishing Branch Conventions

Next, to ensure a clean workflow, we should consider adopting branch naming conventions across the team. For example, we might have branches named **`feature/*`**, **`bugfix/*`**, or **`release/*`** to categorize our work.

Although setting up branches is not part of this immediate step, thinking ahead and aligning on commit and branch conventions within the team will prove invaluable as the grows in complexity and the number of contributors increases.

Configuring Remote Repositories

To link our local repository to a remote server, we will execute this command. In the command below, we will replace **<REMOTE_URL>** with the actual URL of our repository:

```
git remote add origin <REMOTE_URL>
```

It associates our local Git repository with the remote repository, enabling us to push our commits and collaborate with others. After adding the remote, we will push our initial commit to the remote repository. We then run:

```
git push -u origin master
```

This then pushes our local commits to the **`master`** branch of the remote repository and sets up tracking between our local and remote branches, so future pushes and pulls require minimal additional flags.

Ongoing Version Control Practices

As we work on our Laravel project, it is useful to frequently check the status of our repository. We now run this at any point during development:

```
git status
```

It will help us track changes, identify untracked files, and confirm which files are staged for commit. We should also commit regularly as we make changes throughout the project. For example, when adding new features or fixing bugs, we will use descriptive commit messages like the one below:

```
git commit -am "Feature: Add user authentication with Laravel Passport"
```

The **-am** flag allows us to add all modified tracked files and commit them in a single step, which streamlines the workflow considerably. Additionally, we must remember to synchronize our work with teammates by pulling the latest changes before starting any new work. Here, we pull the latest changes:

```
git pull origin master
```

This structured Git setup reinforces the comprehensive environment we are steadily establishing for our Laravel development, and it also sets the stage for future enhancements and smooth team contributions.

Summary

At this point, we just got ourselves with a good foundation for developing Laravel 12 on our Linux environment. We installed PHP 8.5 and the essential extensions, set up Composer to manage our PHP dependencies, and used it to install Laravel 12 without a hitch. We also configured our environment variables, generated the necessary application key, and verified our setup by running the Laravel development server.

We did learn to navigate Laravel's directory structure and set the right Linux file permissions for key folders like **storage** and **bootstrap/cache**, ensuring everything works correctly and remains secure. We also assembled a solid development environment by installing key tools like PhpStorm, Laravel Debugbar, and Telescope, which enhanced our coding, debugging, and system monitoring capabilities. Finally, we set up Git version control for **myapp**, established commit conventions, and connected our local repository to a remote platform so that the team can collaborate and track changes with confidence.

CHAPTER 2

ADVANCED ROUTING, CONTROLLERS, AND BLADE VIEWS

Overview

In this chapter, we will dive into advanced routing techniques, controller logic, and view rendering using Laravel 12. We will learn how to create dynamic routes that respond to user inputs and map them seamlessly to controller methods that handle different data requests. We will also set up a resource controller to streamline CRUD operations, reduce code redundancy, and improve workflow efficiency across our growing **myapp** application.

Further, we will work with Blade templating to pass and render complex, nested dynamic data in our views, making our frontend interactions more adaptive and expressive. Then we will set up API-specific routes and write custom JSON responses to ensure our application can reliably share data with external clients. Each recipe in this chapter builds directly on the Laravel 12 environment we established in Chapter 1, so every step will feel like a natural continuation of what we have already put in place.

Recipe 1: Creating Dynamic Routes and Controller Logic

As we work on our Laravel application **myapp**, we will notice that as the project grows, static routes are no longer sufficient to handle all the different user requests. Dynamic routing becomes essential at this stage. This approach lets our application interpret and process parameters in the URL, directing requests to the right controllers and enabling the application to respond intelligently to varying inputs. In this recipe, we will define dynamic routes in **myapp**, create the corresponding controller logic, and integrate a Blade view to render the output, all building on the setup we completed in Chapter 1.

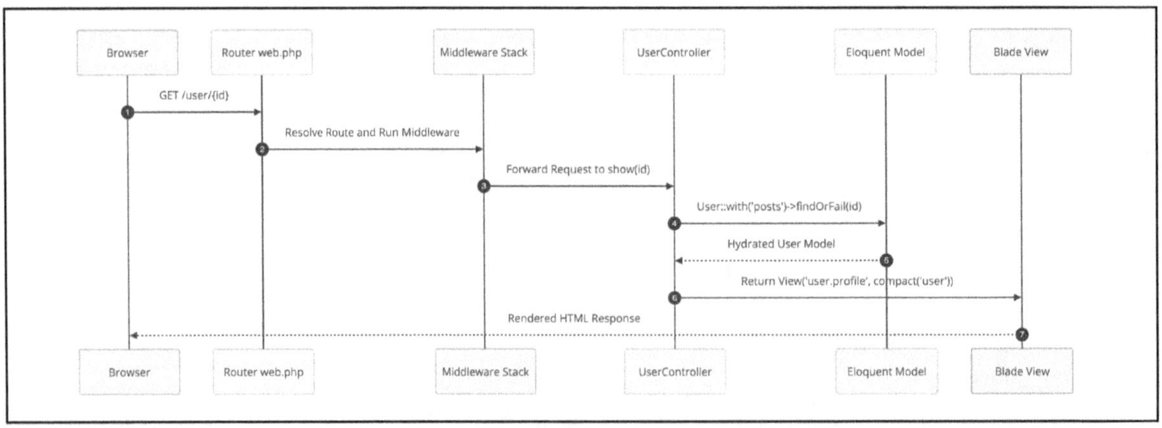

Fig 2.1: Laravel MVC Request Lifecycle

The above lifecycle traces an HTTP request from the browser through the router, middleware, controller, and Eloquent model, all the way back to the rendered view.

Setting up Dynamic Route

To begin, we will navigate to our project directory, open the **`routes/web.php`** file, and we add a new route that captures a dynamic segment from the URL using the following code:

```
Route::get('/user/{id}', [App\Http\Controllers\UserController::class,
'show'])->name('user.show');
```

The **`{id}`** segment in the above URL is dynamic, meaning it can accept any value that represents a user identifier. This configuration directs all GET requests matching **`/user/{id}`** to the **`show`** method within **`UserController`**. The **`->name('user.show')`** call assigns a named route, which allows us to reference this URL from other parts of the application without hardcoding the path, making future refactoring far simpler.

Generating and Editing Controller

Creating UserController

We will now generate the controller using the Artisan command-line tool. At this point, we run:

```
php artisan make:controller UserController
```

This command creates a new file named **`UserController.php`** in the **`app/Http/Controllers`** directory.

```
myapp — -zsh — 80×24

pravindhandre@Pravins-MacBook-Air myapp % php artisan make:controller UserController
 INFO  Controller [app/Http/Controllers/UserController.php] created successfully.
pravindhandre@Pravins-MacBook-Air myapp %
```

Fig 2.2: UserController Created

The Laravel's Artisan scaffolding saves us from manually creating the file and writing boilerplate, ensuring that the controller follows the correct namespace and class structure expected by the framework.

Defining Controller Logic

Next, we will open **`UserController.php`** and define the **`show`** method to handle the dynamic route. We can now update the controller as follows:

```
<?php


namespace App\Http\Controllers;
```

```
use Illuminate\Http\Request;

class UserController extends Controller
{
    /**
     * Display the specified user.
     *
     * @param  int  $id
     * @return \Illuminate\View\View
     */
    public function show($id)
    {
        // For demonstration, we create a mock user array
        $user = [
            'id'    => $id,
            'name'  => 'User ' . $id,
            'email' => 'user' . $id . '@example.com'
        ];

        return view('user.show', compact('user'));
    }
}
```

The **`show`** method accepts the dynamic **`$id`** parameter injected automatically by Laravel's routing layer. It constructs a mock user array using that parameter, then passes the data to the Blade view via **`compact('user')`**. In a production scenario, this is where we would query the database using Eloquent, but for now, this simulated data lets us focus on the routing and rendering mechanics without introducing database complexity ahead of schedule.

Creating Blade View to Render Data

Now, we will navigate to the **`resources/views`** directory and create a new folder named **`user`**. Within that folder, we will create a file called **`show.blade.php`**. From here, we insert the following HTML and Blade code into the file:

```
<!DOCTYPE html>
```

```
<html lang="en">
<head>
    <meta charset="UTF-8">
    <title>User Profile</title>
</head>
<body>
    <h1>User Profile for {{ $user['name'] }}</h1>
    <p>User ID: {{ $user['id'] }}</p>
    <p>Email: {{ $user['email'] }}</p>
</body>
</html>
```

This template uses Blade's double-brace **{{ }}** syntax to safely escape and output each value from the **$user** array. The data flows directly from the controller into this view, so any change to the **$user** array in the controller is immediately reflected in what the browser renders. To test this, we can start the development server with **php artisan serve** and navigate to **http://127.0.0.1:8000/user/1** in our browser. We should see the profile rendered for User 1, which then confirms that our dynamic routing, controller logic, and Blade view are all working together correctly.

Recipe 2: using Resource Controllers for Efficient CRUD Operations

As **myapp** grows more complex, managing CRUD operations individually for different models can lead to repetitive code and disorganized logic. During a team meeting, we realize that a more structured approach is needed. Resource controllers are a built-in Laravel 12 feature that organizes all CRUD-related methods into a single, coherent controller. This approach keeps our codebase clean, accelerates development, and simplifies maintenance as we continue to build out the application. In this recipe, we will generate a resource controller, understand its auto-generated methods, and wire it up with a single resource route.

Creating Resource Controller

To start, we will generate a resource controller for a **Product** model in our application. So here, we will then run this Artisan command from the **myapp** directory:

```
php artisan make:controller ProductController --resource
```

It creates a new file named **ProductController.php** in the **app/Http/Controllers** directory.

```
myapp — -zsh — 80×24

pravindhandre@Pravins-MacBook-Air myapp % php artisan make:controller ProductController --resource
 INFO  Controller [app/Http/Controllers/ProductController.php] created successfully.
pravindhandre@Pravins-MacBook-Air myapp %
```

Fig 2.3: ProductController Resource

The **--resource** flag instructs Artisan to pre-populate the controller with all seven standard CRUD methods rather than generating an empty class. This automatic scaffolding means we can move directly to writing business logic instead of spending time on structural boilerplate.

Resource Controller Methods

Upon opening **ProductController.php**, we will observe seven pre-built methods that together cover the full lifecycle of a resource. The **index()** method lists all products, while **create()** displays the form for adding a new one. The **store()** method processes that form submission and persists the new product. For viewing, editing, and updating existing records, we have **show($id)**, **edit($id)**, and **update($id)** respectively. Finally, **destroy($id)** handles deletion. Each method is designed to handle a specific and well-scoped responsibility, keeping our controller focused and easy to extend as requirements evolve.

Defining Resource Routes

Now, we will wire up all seven controller methods with a single route declaration. So here, we will then open **routes/web.php** and add the following line:

```
Route::resource('products',
App\Http\Controllers\ProductController::class);
```

This single line automatically maps the standard HTTP verbs GET, POST, PUT/PATCH, and DELETE to their corresponding methods in **ProductController**. The framework handles the URL pattern generation and method mapping for us, so we do not need to declare seven separate route entries. This efficient approach also enforces consistent endpoint naming conventions across the application, making the API surface of our web routes predictable and easy to audit as **myapp** scales.

Recipe 3: Rendering Blade Templates with Dynamic Data

As we continue developing **myapp**, we face a challenge where rendering static content is no longer sufficient. The information displayed must become increasingly complex and dynamic, responding to backend data and user interactions. In a recent team meeting, we discussed the need to display rich product details including images, features, and prices in a clear, structured format.

In this recipe, we will work with Blade templates to pass and render intricate data structures from our controllers to our views, leveraging the full power of Laravel's built-in templating engine.

Blade Templates Overview

Blade is Laravel's intuitive templating engine that allows us to write clean, expressive syntax for our HTML. It provides directives for control structures, loops, and data binding, streamlining the rendering of dynamic content. All Blade templates live in the **`resources/views`** directory and use the **`.blade.php`** extension. This convention means we can freely mix PHP logic and HTML markup while keeping the template layer separate from our application logic. We will now see how these capabilities allow us to render complex data models passed down from our controllers in a maintainable and readable way.

Passing Complex Data from Controller

We will now modify **`ProductController`** to pass a rich, nested product dataset to a Blade view. So here, we will then open **`ProductController.php`** and update the **`index()`** method as follows:

```
<?php

namespace App\Http\Controllers;

use Illuminate\Http\Request;

class ProductController extends Controller
{
    /**
     * Display a listing of the products.
     *
     * @return \Illuminate\View\View
     */
    public function index()
    {
        $products = [
            [
                'id'        => 1,
```

```
            'name'      => 'Smartphone Model X',
            'price'     => 699.99,
            'features' => [
                'Display' => '6.1 inch OLED',
                'Battery' => '3700 mAh',
                'Camera'  => '12 MP dual rear camera'
            ],
            'images' => [
                'front' => 'modelx-front.jpg',
                'back'  => 'modelx-back.jpg'
            ]
        ],
        [
            'id'        => 2,
            'name'      => 'Laptop Pro 15',
            'price'     => 1299.99,
            'features' => [
                'Display'   => '15.6 inch Retina',
                'Processor' => 'Intel i7',
                'Memory'    => '16 GB'
            ],
            'images' => [
                'front' => 'laptoppro-front.jpg',
                'side'  => 'laptoppro-side.jpg'
            ]
        ]
    ];

    return view('products.index', compact('products'));
  }
}
```

The **$products** array holds two items, each containing nested sub-arrays for **features** and **images**. This structure mirrors the kind of complex, relational data our application will eventually pull from a database. By passing this array through **compact('products')**, we make the entire nested structure available inside the Blade view under the variable name **$products**. This data-passing pattern scales naturally, so as we connect real Eloquent models in later chapters, this same controller structure will continue to work without modification.

Creating Blade View to Render Dynamic Data

Now that the controller is supplying complex data to the view, we will create a Blade file to iterate over and display it. So here, we will then create the file at **resources/views/products/index.blade.php** and populate it:

```
<!DOCTYPE html>
<html lang="en">
<head>
    <meta charset="UTF-8">
    <title>Product Listings</title>
</head>
<body>
    <h1>Product Listings</h1>

    @foreach ($products as $product)
    <div style="border: 1px solid #ccc; padding: 15px; margin-bottom:
15px;">
        <h2>{{ $product['name'] }} (ID: {{ $product['id'] }})</h2>
        <p>Price: ${{ number_format($product['price'], 2) }}</p>

        <h3>Features:</h3>
        <ul>
            @foreach ($product['features'] as $key => $value)
                <li><strong>{{ $key }}:</strong> {{ $value }}</li>
            @endforeach
        </ul>

        <h3>Images:</h3>
```

```
        <ul>
            @foreach ($product['images'] as $view => $filename)
                <li>{{ ucfirst($view) }} View:
                    <img src="/images/{{ $filename }}"
                         alt="{{ $product['name'] }} {{ $view }}"
                         width="100">
                </li>
            @endforeach
        </ul>
    </div>
    @endforeach
</body>
</html>
```

This view uses Blade's **@foreach** directive to iterate over the outer **$products** array and, for each product, two additional nested loops render the **features** and **images** sub-arrays. The **number_format()** helper formats the price to two decimal places, and **ucfirst()** capitalizes the image view label. Because the template is entirely data-driven, any additions to the **$products** array in the controller are automatically reflected in the rendered output without any change to the HTML structure. This separation of data from presentation is one of Blade's most valuable properties as the application grows.

Recipe 4: Designing API Routes and Custom JSON Responses

While working on **myapp**, we notice that standard web responses are not meeting the needs of external clients or mobile applications. The current responses lack consistent formatting, making it difficult for consumers to reliably parse data. In a team meeting, we agree that organizing API responses with a clean, predictable structure is essential. In this recipe, we will scaffold the API layer in Laravel 12, define API-specific routes, and craft custom JSON responses that provide a reliable data format for any client consuming our endpoints.

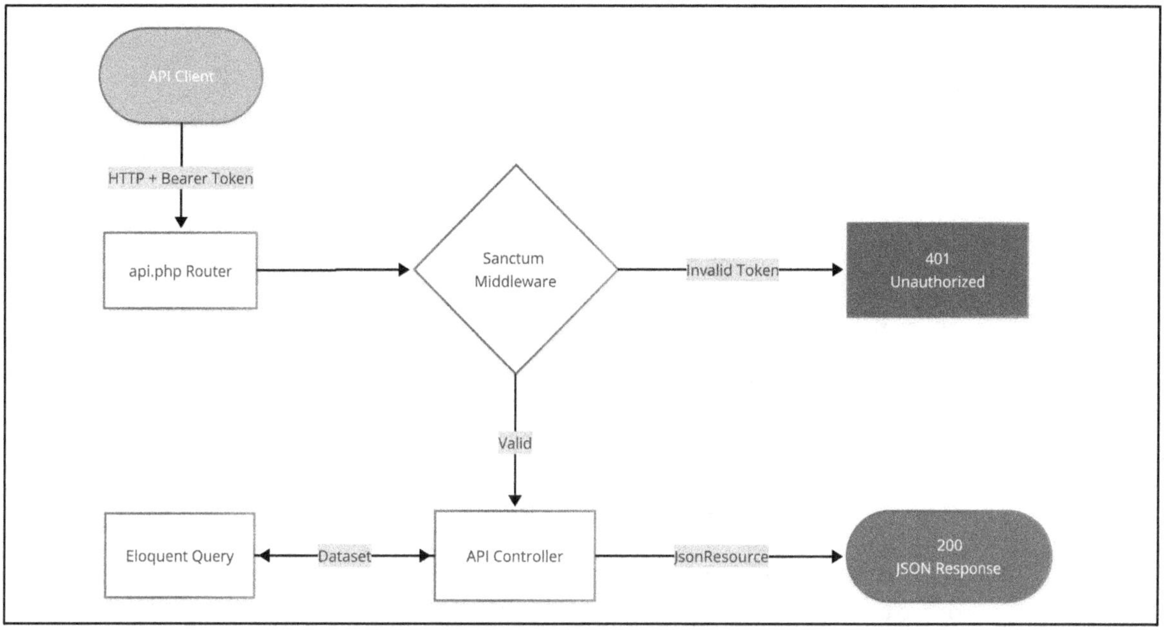

Fig 2.4: API Request and Response Flow

The above flow diagram shows an API request is authenticated by Sanctum, handled by the controller, and returned as a JSON resource, including the failure branch when the token is missing or invalid.

Scaffolding API Layer in Laravel 12

In Laravel 12, the **`routes/api.php`** file is not created by default and must be explicitly scaffolded. So here, we will then run this Artisan command from the **`myapp`** directory:

```
php artisan install:api
```

The terminal will confirm the scaffolding as shown below:

```
INFO  API scaffolding installed. Please add the
[Laravel\Sanctum\HasApiTokens] trait to your User model.
```

This command creates **`routes/api.php`**, registers the API route file with the application's bootstrap configuration, and installs Laravel Sanctum for token-based API authentication.

```
myapp — -zsh — 80×24

pravindhandre@Pravins-MacBook-Air myapp % php artisan install:api
 INFO  Published API routes file.

   One new database migration has been published. Would you like to
   run all pending database migrations? (yes/no) [yes]:
   > yes

 INFO  Running migrations.
  2026_05_09_053657_create_personal_access_tokens_table ...... 5.76ms DONE

 INFO  API scaffolding installed. Please add the [Laravel\Sanctum\HasApiTokens]
trait to your User model.
pravindhandre@Pravins-MacBook-Air myapp %
```

Fig 2.5: API Scaffold Installed

All routes defined in **`routes/api.php`** will automatically be prefixed with **`/api`**, so a route declared as **`/products`** will be accessible at **`http://127.0.0.1:8000/api/products`**. This clean separation ensures our API logic remains isolated from our web routes.

Defining API-specific Routes

With the API layer in place, we will now open **`routes/api.php`** and add a route that maps to a dedicated API controller. We then add the following route declaration:

```
Route::get('/products',
[App\Http\Controllers\Api\ProductApiController::class, 'index'])

    ->name('api.products.index');
```

This route listens for GET requests to **`/api/products`** and directs them to the **`index`** method in **`ProductApiController`**, placed under the **`App\Http\Controllers\Api`** namespace. Keeping API controllers in a dedicated **`Api`** subdirectory separates them from our web controllers, making the codebase easier to navigate and maintain as the number of endpoints grows.

Generating API Controller

We will now generate the dedicated API controller using Artisan. We now run:

```
php artisan make:controller Api/ProductApiController
```

It creates the file **`app/Http/Controllers/Api/ProductApiController.php`**. Laravel automatically creates the **`Api`** subdirectory if it does not already exist.

```
myapp — -zsh — 80×24
pravindhandre@Pravins-MacBook-Air myapp % php artisan make:controller Api/ProductApiController
 INFO  Controller [app/Http/Controllers/Api/ProductApiController.php] created successfully.
pravindhandre@Pravins-MacBook-Air myapp %
```

Fig 2.6: ProductApiController Created

When we place the API controllers in their own namespace and directory, it helps to keep our API logic self-contained and prevents it from becoming entangled with the view-rendering logic that lives in our standard web controllers.

Adding Custom JSON Response Logic

Now, we will open the newly created **`ProductApiController.php`** and define the **`index`** method. Here, we build out the controller with the following code:

```
<?php

namespace App\Http\Controllers\Api;

use App\Http\Controllers\Controller;
use Illuminate\Http\Request;

class ProductApiController extends Controller
{
    /**
     * Return a structured JSON response for products.
     *
     * @return \Illuminate\Http\JsonResponse
     */
    public function index()
    {
        $products = [
            [
                'id'        => 1,
                'name'      => 'Smartphone Model X',
                'price'     => 699.99,
```

```
                'features' => [
                    'Display' => '6.1 inch OLED',
                    'Battery' => '3700 mAh',
                    'Camera'  => '12 MP dual rear camera'
                ]
            ],
            [
                'id'       => 2,
                'name'     => 'Laptop Pro 15',
                'price'    => 1299.99,
                'features' => [
                    'Display'   => '15.6 inch Retina',
                    'Processor' => 'Intel i7',
                    'Memory'    => '16 GB'
                ]
            ]
        ];

        $response = [
            'success' => true,
            'data'    => $products,
            'message' => 'Products fetched successfully.',
        ];

        return response()->json($response, 200);
    }
}
```

The **index** method constructs a **$response** array with three explicit keys. The **success** key is a boolean flag indicating the status of the request. The **data** key carries the actual product payload, and the **message** key provides a human-readable status string that consumers can display or log. Returning this structure with **response()->json($response, 200)** ensures that the HTTP status code and the **Content-Type: application/json** header are both set correctly by Laravel. Any client consuming this endpoint will always receive the same predictable envelope regardless of how the underlying data changes.

Verifying Custom JSON Response

Now, we will confirm that our API endpoint is functioning correctly for which, we will first start the development server:

```
php artisan serve
```

Once the server is running, we can open a browser or an API testing tool such as Postman and navigate to **`http://127.0.0.1:8000/api/products`**. The terminal output below confirms the server is ready:

```
INFO  Server running on [http://127.0.0.1:8000].


  Press Ctrl+C to stop the server
```

We should see a well-structured JSON response containing our sample products, the **`success`** flag, and the status message. This confirms that our API route, controller, and response structure are all configured correctly and working as expected in **`myapp`**.

Summary

In this chapter, we worked through the core building blocks of Laravel's web and API architecture. We started by creating dynamic routes that captured URL segments and mapped them to controller methods, allowing **`myapp`** to process user requests intelligently. We then generated a **`UserController`** using Artisan and defined the logic to handle dynamic parameters, connecting it to a Blade view for rendering. Moving forward, we implemented a resource controller to streamline CRUD operations, replacing multiple individual route definitions with a single, concise **`Route::resource`** declaration.

We then worked with Blade templating to pass complex, nested data structures from **`ProductController`** to a view, using **`@foreach`** directives to render rich product details dynamically. Finally, we scaffolded the API layer using **`php artisan install:api`**, defined API-specific routes in **`routes/api.php`**, created a dedicated API controller, and returned custom JSON responses with a consistent envelope structure. Every step in this chapter builds on the Laravel 12 environment from Chapter 1 and prepares **`myapp`** for the more advanced data modeling and database work ahead.

CHAPTER 3

AUTHENTICATION AND AUTHORIZATION

Overview

In this chapter, we will work on making **myapp** more secure by strengthening how users are verified and what they can access. We will integrate Laravel Breeze to establish a secure baseline for user login, registration, and password management. We will also implement role-based access control using custom middleware to clearly define and enforce access hierarchies for different user roles across the application.

Further, we will integrate social login functionality using Laravel Socialite, allowing users to register and sign in via their preferred social platforms. To add an extra layer of security, we will enable two-factor authentication with Laravel Fortify, protecting user accounts from unauthorized access. Each recipe in this chapter builds on our project and the Laravel 12 environment we set up in Chapter 1, adding progressively more robust security features with every step.

Recipe 1: Building Secure User Authentication

There will come a point in every application's life where securing user access becomes non-negotiable. In a busy team meeting for **myapp**, we discussed the potential security risks and agreed that implementing robust user authentication is essential to protecting sensitive data and managing user sessions correctly. We have chosen Laravel Breeze, a lightweight authentication starter kit, to ensure that user logins, registrations, and password management are handled securely from the start. Breeze provides all the essential routes, controllers, and views needed to support login, registration, password reset, and email verification out of the box.

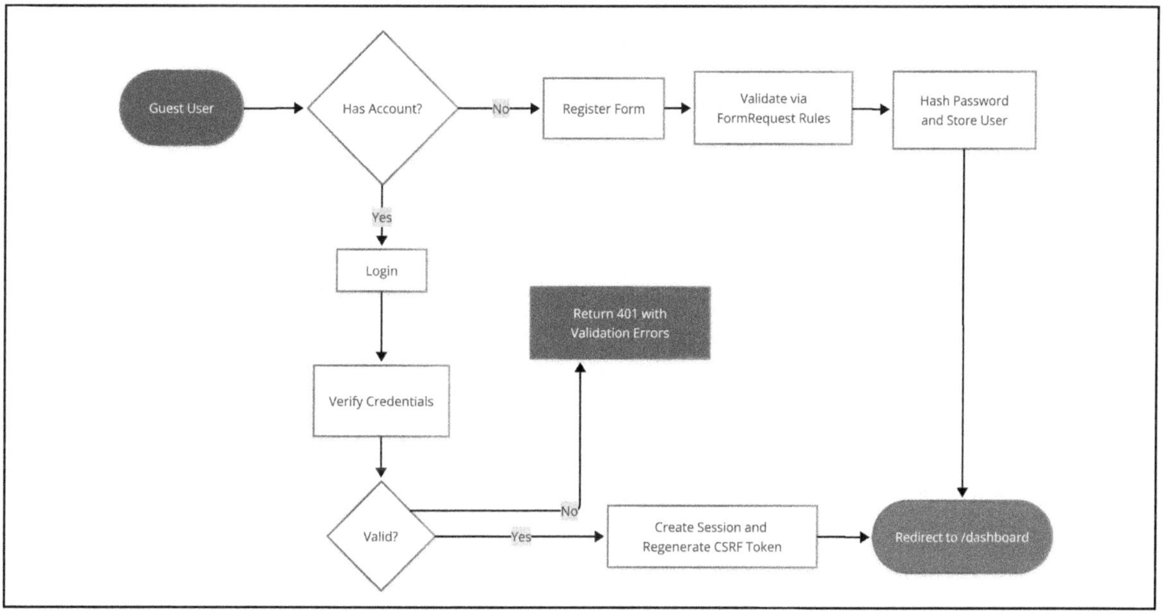

Fig3.1: Breeze Authentication Flow

The above flowchart details both the registration and login paths side by side. It shows, very clearly, how every branch flows from a guest visit through to a fully authenticated session.

Installing Laravel Breeze

At this point, we pull Laravel Breeze as a development dependency:

```
composer require laravel/breeze --dev
```

The composer resolves the Breeze package and its front-end scaffolding dependencies without any conflicts:

```
myapp — -zsh — 80×24

pravindhandre@Pravins-MacBook-Air myapp % composer require laravel/breeze --dev
 INFO  Discovering packages.
  barryvdh/laravel-debugbar ........................................ DONE
  laravel/breeze ................................................... DONE
  laravel/pail ..................................................... DONE
  laravel/sanctum .................................................. DONE
  laravel/telescope ................................................ DONE
  laravel/tinker ................................................... DONE
  nesbot/carbon .................................................... DONE
  nunomaduro/collision ............................................. DONE
  nunomaduro/termwind .............................................. DONE
83 packages you are using are looking for funding.
No security vulnerability advisories found.
Using version ^2.4 for laravel/breeze
pravindhandre@Pravins-MacBook-Air myapp %
```

Fig 3.2: Breeze Installed

Once the package is installed, we will initialize Breeze:

```
php artisan breeze:install
```

This then scaffolds all authentication routes, controllers, and views within **`myapp`**.

```
myapp — -zsh — 80×24
pravindhandre@Pravins-MacBook-Air myapp % php artisan breeze:install

  Which Breeze stack would you like to install?
  Blade with Alpine .................................... blade
  > blade

  Would you prefer Pest or PHPUnit for testing? [PHPUnit]:
  > PHPUnit

vite v7.3.3 building client environment for production...
  55 modules transformed.
  public/build/manifest.json    0.33 kB  | gzip:   0.16 kB
  public/build/assets/app-DnIt7Yfk.css  36.19 kB  | gzip:  6.76 kB
  public/build/assets/app-DsIK1Lmc.js   88.21 kB  | gzip: 32.61 kB
  built in 818ms

 INFO  Breeze scaffolding installed successfully.
pravindhandre@Pravins-MacBook-Air myapp %
```

Fig 3.3: Breeze Scaffolded

The Breeze also sets up Tailwind CSS and the supporting frontend assets used in the authentication views. We can now install and compile those assets:

```
npm install && npm run dev
```

Running Migrations and Testing Authentication

Before testing the authentication flows, we will need to create the necessary database tables for user management. From here, we run the migrations:

```
php artisan migrate
```

Once completed, we will start the development server with **`php artisan serve`** and visit the application in the browser. We should now see ready-to-use login, registration, and password reset pages, all confirming that Breeze has been wired up correctly within our project.

Recipe 2: Implementing Role-Based Access Control

As **`myapp`** expands to include sensitive areas that require controlled access, we need to ensure that only authorized users can reach certain endpoints. During a strategy session, our team decides to implement role-based access control (RBAC) using roles such as **`admin`**, **`editor`**, and **`user`**. In Laravel 12, the middleware registration no longer uses **`app/Http/Kernel.php`**. Instead, all middleware aliases are registered directly inside **bootstrap/app.php** via the **withMiddleware** callback, which is an important architectural shift from earlier versions of the framework.

The decision tree below traces every check the RoleMiddleware performs before granting or denying access, making it easy to reason about edge cases before writing any code:

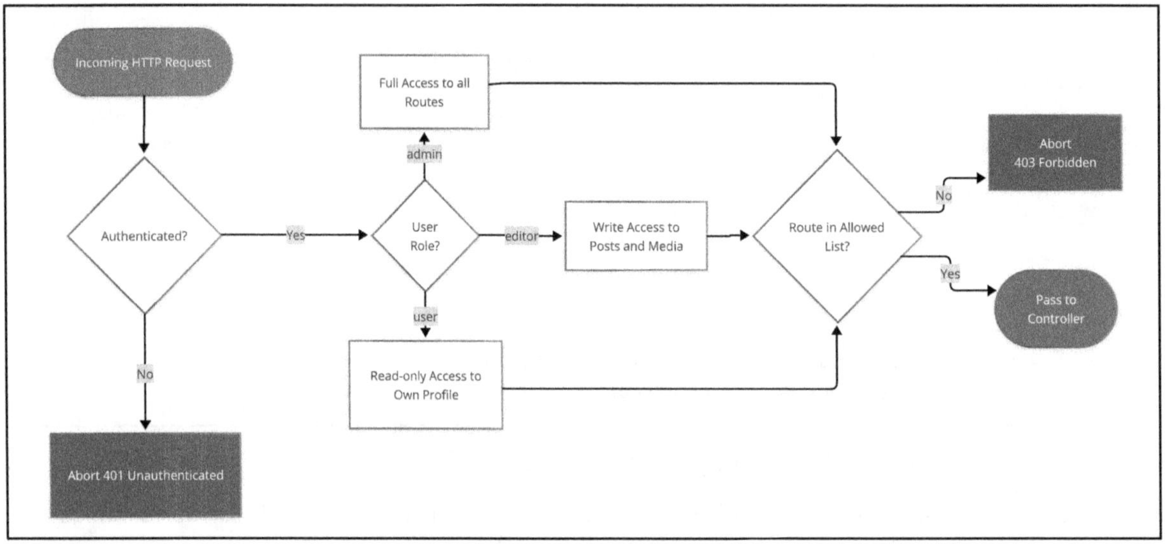

Fig3.4: RBAC Middleware Decision Tree

Creating Custom Middleware

We then generate our role-checking middleware:

```
php artisan make:middleware RoleMiddleware
```

The generated middleware stub is in place and ready to receive the role-checking logic we will add next:

Fig 3.5: CheckUserRole Middleware Created

This creates a new file at **app/Http/Middleware/RoleMiddleware.php**. We will then open that file and update the **handle** method with the following logic:

```php
<?php

namespace App\Http\Middleware;

use Closure;
use Illuminate\Http\Request;
use Illuminate\Support\Facades\Auth;

class RoleMiddleware
{
    public function handle(Request $request, Closure $next, string
...$roles): mixed
    {
        if (!Auth::check()) {
            return redirect('/login');
        }

        if (!in_array(Auth::user()->role, $roles)) {
            abort(403, 'Unauthorized action.');
        }

        return $next($request);
    }
}
```

The **handle** method accepts a variadic **$roles** parameter, which means we can pass one or multiple permitted roles when applying this middleware to a route. If the authenticated user's **role** attribute does not appear in that list, the request is immediately halted with a **403** response. This single method covers both simple single-role checks and more complex permission hierarchies without requiring separate middleware classes.

Registering Middleware in Laravel 12

In Laravel 12, we register custom middleware aliases inside **bootstrap/app.php**. We now open that file and update it as follows:

```
->withMiddleware(function (Middleware $middleware) {
    $middleware->alias([
        'role' => \App\Http\Middleware\RoleMiddleware::class,
    ]);
})
```

This registers the **role** alias for our middleware, making it available to apply to any route or route group throughout **myapp**. This approach replaces the **$routeMiddleware** array that existed in **app/Http/Kernel.php** in older versions of Laravel, so it is important to ensure we are using this bootstrap-based registration pattern when working with Laravel 12.

Applying Middleware to Routes

Now, we will enforce role-based access control on our routes. So here, we will then open **routes/web.php** and add the following protected route groups:

```
Route::group(['middleware' => ['auth', 'role:admin']], function () {
    Route::get('/admin/dashboard',
[App\Http\Controllers\AdminController::class, 'dashboard'])
        ->name('admin.dashboard');
});


Route::group(['middleware' => ['auth', 'role:admin,editor']], function
() {
    Route::get('/management',
[App\Http\Controllers\ManagementController::class, 'index'])
        ->name('management.index');
});
```

The first group restricts access to users with the **admin** role only. The second group permits both **admin** and **editor** users, demonstrating the variadic role-checking we implemented in the middleware. This pattern gives us a clean, scalable way to define permission hierarchies across all of **myapp**'s protected sections.

Recipe 3: Integrating Social Logins

After reviewing user feedback, we realize that traditional authentication alone is not sufficient for our growing user base. Our team agrees that offering social media login options will simplify the registration process and attract a broader audience. We will leverage Laravel Socialite, a package that abstracts the complexity of OAuth authentication, to allow users to sign in using platforms like GitHub.

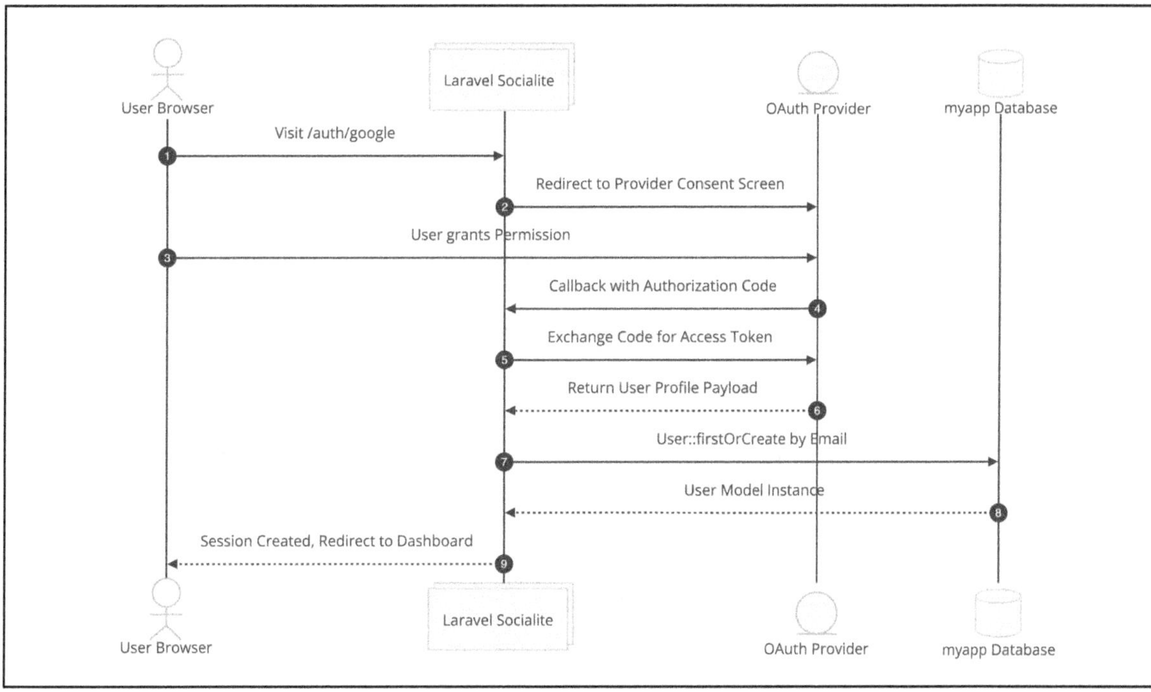

Fig 3.6: OAuth Social Login via Socialite

The above sequence diagram shows the full eight-step OAuth handshake that happens between the browser, Laravel Socialite, the external provider, and the database each time a user signs in socially.

In this recipe, we will install Socialite, configure it for GitHub, and set up the routes and controller methods that handle the redirect and the OAuth callback within **`myapp`**.

Installing Laravel Socialite

Here, we install Socialite:

```
composer require laravel/socialite
```

The Laravel automatically registers Socialite through package auto-discovery, so no manual provider registration is required in **`config/app.php`**.

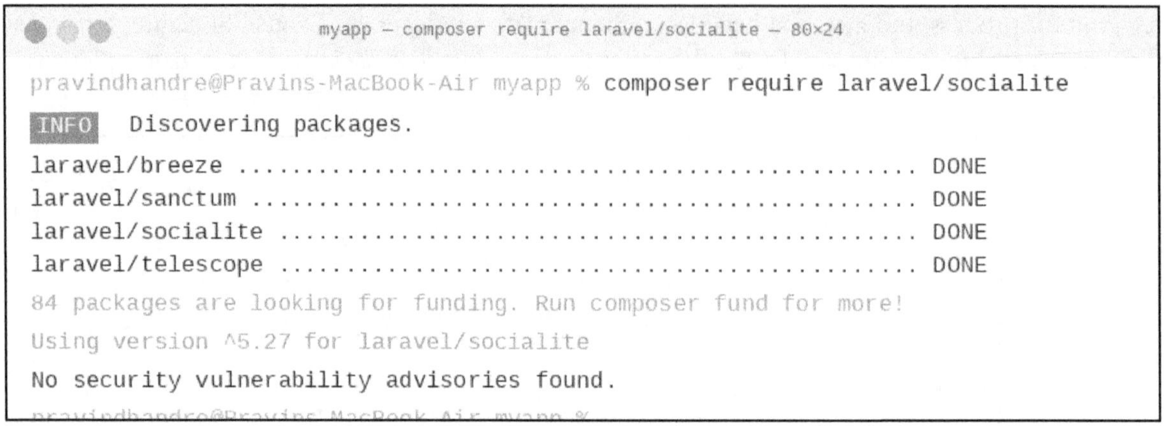

Fig 3.7: Socialite Installed

Configuring Socialite for GitHub

We will configure the GitHub provider by opening **config/services.php** and adding the following entry:

```
'github' => [
    'client_id'     => env('GITHUB_CLIENT_ID'),
    'client_secret' => env('GITHUB_CLIENT_SECRET'),
    'redirect'      => env('GITHUB_REDIRECT_URI'),
],
```

Next, we will update the **.env** file with the credentials obtained from our GitHub OAuth app registration:

```
GITHUB_CLIENT_ID=your_github_client_id
GITHUB_CLIENT_SECRET=your_github_client_secret
GITHUB_REDIRECT_URI=http://127.0.0.1:8000/auth/github/callback
```

Setting up Social Auth Controller and Routes

We will now generate the controller that manages the social authentication flow:

```
php artisan make:controller SocialAuthController
```

After the file is created, we will open it and add two methods as shown below:

```
<?php
```

```
namespace App\Http\Controllers;

use Laravel\Socialite\Facades\Socialite;

class SocialAuthController extends Controller
{
    public function redirectToProvider()
    {
        return Socialite::driver('github')->redirect();
    }

    public function handleProviderCallback()
    {
        $githubUser = Socialite::driver('github')->user();

        // Find or create a local user record using $githubUser-
>getEmail()
        // and $githubUser->getName() before issuing a session.

        return response()->json($githubUser);
    }
}
```

The **redirectToProvider** method sends the user to GitHub's OAuth authorization page. Once the user grants permission, GitHub redirects them back to our callback URL, where **handleProviderCallback** retrieves the authenticated GitHub user object. The **$githubUser** instance exposes methods like **getEmail()**, **getName()**, and **token**, which we use to find or create the matching local user in our database. Finally, we will then add the two corresponding routes to **routes/web.php**:

```
Route::get('/auth/github',
[App\Http\Controllers\SocialAuthController::class,
'redirectToProvider'])
    ->name('auth.github');
```

```
Route::get('/auth/github/callback',
[App\Http\Controllers\SocialAuthController::class,
'handleProviderCallback'])
    ->name('auth.github.callback');
```

At this point, our OAuth flow is fully operational within the Laravel 12 application. Once a user clicks the social login button, they will be redirected to the provider, and upon approval, our callback controller will retrieve their profile, locate or create the matching local user record, and then establish an authenticated session. We will now find that social authentication integrates cleanly alongside the Breeze-based credential login we configured earlier in this chapter, giving our users a flexible and secure sign-in experience.

Recipe 4: Enforcing Two-Factor Authentication

With secure user authentication, social logins, and role-based access control already in place, we will now learn to add an additional layer of protection to **myapp** through two-factor authentication (2FA). For example, let us say that, during a review meeting, the team agreed that 2FA is essential for preventing unauthorized account access even when credentials are compromised.

So in this recipe, we will implement it using Laravel Fortify, which integrates seamlessly with the authentication infrastructure we have already established and provides first-class support for time-based one-time password (TOTP) 2FA out of the box.

Installing Laravel Fortify

So here, we will first install Fortify from our project directory:

```
composer require laravel/fortify
```

The Fortify arrives as a headless authentication backend, shipping no UI of its own and giving us full control over views:

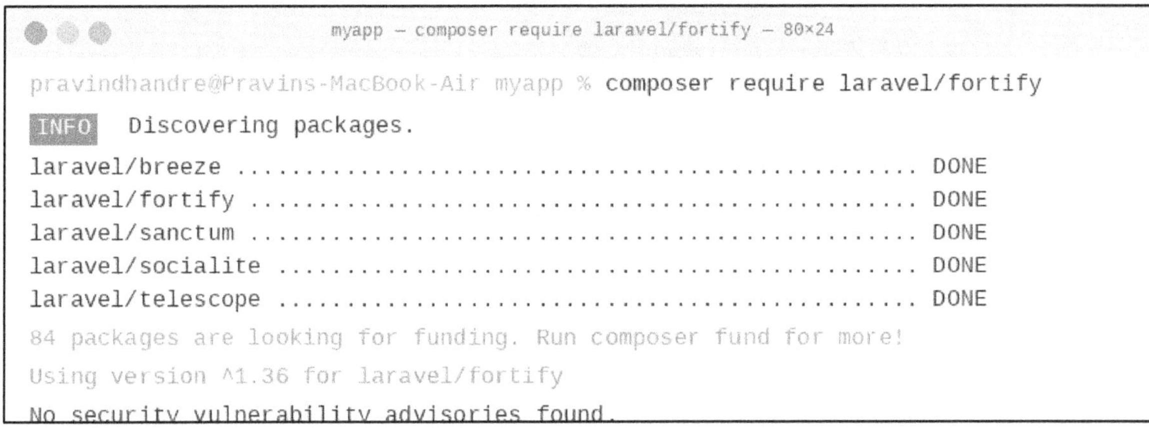

Fig 3.8: Fortify Installed

Once installed, we will publish Fortify's configuration file:

```
php artisan vendor:publish --
provider="Laravel\Fortify\FortifyServiceProvider"
```

This creates a **config/fortify.php** file where we can manage all authentication feature flags, including two-factor authentication.

Configuring Two-Factor Authentication

To store 2FA credentials, the **users** table needs two additional columns. At this point, we create a new migration and add the required fields as follows:

```
Schema::table('users', function (Blueprint $table) {
    $table->text('two_factor_secret')->nullable();
    $table->text('two_factor_recovery_codes')->nullable();
});
```

After saving the migration file, we will run it with **php artisan migrate**.

And then, we will open **app/Models/User.php** and apply **TwoFactorAuthenticatable** trait provided by Fortify:

```
use Laravel\Fortify\TwoFactorAuthenticatable;

class User extends Authenticatable
{
    use TwoFactorAuthenticatable;
```

```
    // ...
}
```

This trait wires the user model into Fortify's 2FA infrastructure, enabling the generation and validation of TOTP codes and recovery codes for each user account.

Enabling 2FA Feature Flag

We will now confirm that 2FA is enabled in Fortify's configuration. So here, we will then open **config/fortify.php** and verify that the **features** array includes the following entry:

```
'features' => [
    // other features...
    Features::twoFactorAuthentication([
        'confirmPassword' => true,
    ]),
],
```

The **confirmPassword** option ensures that users must re-enter their password before enabling or disabling 2FA on their account, adding an important safeguard against unauthorized configuration changes. With this in place, we can start the server with **php artisan serve**, log in to **myapp**, and navigate to the user profile settings where the two-factor authentication options will now appear. The on-screen flow will guide the user through scanning a QR code with an authenticator app such as Google Authenticator, and recovery codes will be generated for secure storage.

Summary

Throughout this chapter, we worked on securing myapp with a layered authentication and authorization system. We began by integrating Laravel Breeze to establish a reliable user authentication flow covering login, registration, and password reset. We then implemented RBAC by creating custom middleware that verifies user roles, registering it using Laravel 12's bootstrap/app.php middleware alias approach, and applying it to protected route groups.

Next, we integrated social logins via Laravel Socialite, giving users the option to authenticate using their GitHub account through a clean redirect-and-callback flow. Finally, we introduced two-factor authentication using Laravel Fortify, adding the necessary database columns, applying the TwoFactorAuthenticatable trait to the user model, and enabling the 2FA feature flag in Fortify's configuration. Each recipe in this chapter strengthens a different layer of myapp's security model, and all of them build naturally on the foundation established in Chapters 1 and 2.

CHAPTER 4
DATABASE MODELS, MIGRATIONS, AND QUERY OPTIMIZATION

Overview

In this chapter, we will design, set up, and optimize the database layer of **myapp** so that it can adapt to the application's evolving needs. We will build Eloquent models that handle one-to-many and many-to-many relationships, enabling clean and efficient data retrieval. We will also create and execute migration files using Artisan, ensuring that our database schema evolves in a version-controlled, team-friendly way.

Beyond schema management, we will explore data seeding and model factories to generate consistent, realistic datasets for development and testing. We will then tackle query performance by addressing the N+1 problem through eager loading, verify improvements with Laravel Debugbar, and extend our toolkit further with two additional recipes covering dynamic test data generation with factories and reusable query logic with Eloquent scopes. Together, these techniques give us a cohesive and scalable approach to managing **myapp**'s entire data layer.

Recipe 1: Defining Database Models and Relationships

As **myapp** grows, we need to model how data entities relate to one another with precision. Each user should be able to write multiple posts, representing a one-to-many relationship. Each post can be associated with several tags, and each tag can belong to multiple posts, forming a many-to-many relationship. We will also establish that each post can have multiple comments, which we will use when optimizing queries in a later recipe.

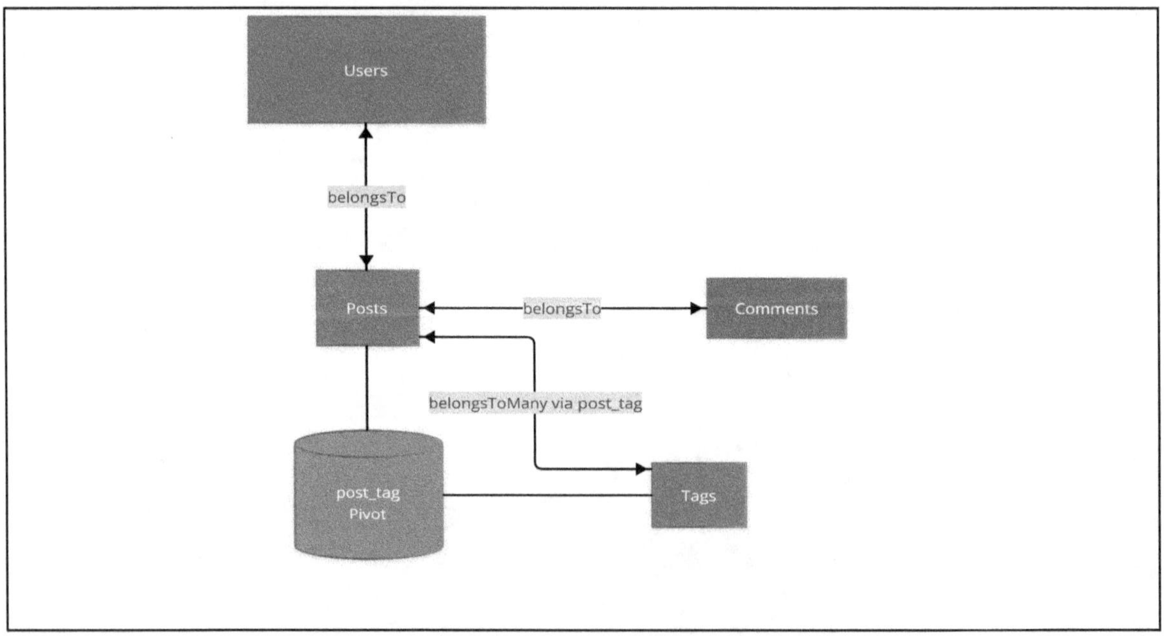

Fig 4.1: Eloquent Model Relationships

The diagram above maps every relationship between the four core models so you can see the cardinality and direction before writing a single line of migration code.

Creating Models and Migrations

So here, we will then generate the **`Post`**, **`Tag`**, and **`Comment`** models along with their migration files:

```
php artisan make:model Post -m

php artisan make:model Tag -m

php artisan make:model Comment -m
```

Here, the Artisan generates both the Eloquent model and a paired migration file in one pass:

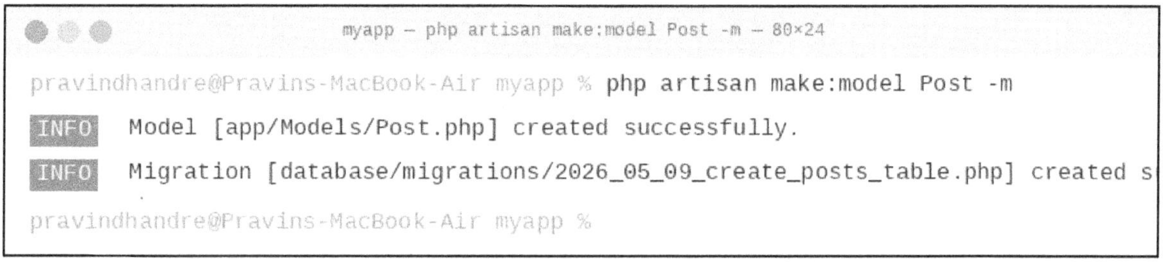

Fig 4.2: Post Model Created

Defining One-to-Many Relationships

We will now open **`app/Models/User.php`** and add the **`posts`** relationship method as shown below:

```
public function posts()
{
    return $this->hasMany(Post::class);
}
```

Next, we will open **`app/Models/Post.php`** and define both the inverse relationship back to the user and the one-to-many relationship down to comments:

```
protected $fillable = ['title', 'content', 'user_id'];


public function user()
{
    return $this->belongsTo(User::class);
```

```
}

public function comments()
{
    return $this->hasMany(Comment::class);
}
```

Then, we will open **app/Models/Comment.php** and add the inverse relationship:

```
protected $fillable = ['post_id', 'author', 'content'];

public function post()
{
    return $this->belongsTo(Post::class);
}
```

Defining Many-to-Many Relationship

We will now add the tag associations to **Post** and **Tag**. So here, we will then open **app/Models/Post.php** and add the following method:

```
public function tags()
{
    return $this->belongsToMany(Tag::class);
}
```

Then, we will open **app/Models/Tag.php** and define the reciprocal method:

```
protected $fillable = ['name'];

public function posts()
{
    return $this->belongsToMany(Post::class);
}
```

Creating Pivot Table Migration

The many-to-many relationship between posts and tags requires a dedicated pivot table. We can now generate that migration:

```
php artisan make:migration create_post_tag_table --create=post_tag
```

Once executed, the migrations apply all pending schema changes to the SQLite database in sequence. We will then open the generated migration file and define the pivot schema as follows:

```
public function up(): void
{
    Schema::create('post_tag', function (Blueprint $table) {
        $table->id();
        $table->foreignId('post_id')->constrained()-
>onDelete('cascade');
        $table->foreignId('tag_id')->constrained()-
>onDelete('cascade');
        $table->timestamps();
    });
}

public function down(): void
{
    Schema::dropIfExists('post_tag');
}
```

The **`constrained()`** method automatically references the **`posts`** and **`tags`** tables respectively, and **`onDelete('cascade')`** ensures that pivot records are removed whenever the parent post or tag is deleted, keeping our database clean and consistent. Finally, we will run the migrations to create all the necessary tables:

```
php artisan migrate
```

With these relationships in place, our models are now fully connected through the foreign keys defined in the migrations we ran earlier in this chapter. We will now be able to call **`$post->comments`** to retrieve all related records, or call **`$comment->post`** to traverse back to the parent. At this stage, Eloquent resolves these associations automatically, and we can chain further query constraints, apply **`where`** clauses, or eager load them using **`with()`** to keep our database queries efficient and our controllers clean.

Recipe 2: Creating and Executing Migrations

Version-controlled schema changes are a cornerstone of a well-managed Laravel project. Our team agreed that having migration files for every schema change means the entire team can synchronize database structure without manual SQL scripts or environment-specific discrepancies. In this recipe, we will generate a migration for the **comments** table, customize the schema, and work through the essential Artisan commands for executing and inspecting migrations in our Linux environment.

Generating and Customizing Migration

In Recipe 1, we generated the **Comment** model and its migration together. We will now open the **create_comments_table** migration file located in the **database/migrations** directory and define the schema. So here, we will then update the **up** method as follows:

```
public function up(): void
{
    Schema::create('comments', function (Blueprint $table) {
        $table->id();
        $table->foreignId('post_id')->constrained()-
>onDelete('cascade');
        $table->string('author');
        $table->text('content');
        $table->timestamps();
    });
}

public function down(): void
{
    Schema::dropIfExists('comments');
}
```

This schema sets up a **comments** table with a primary key, a cascading foreign key to the **posts** table, an **author** string column, a **content** text column, and automatic timestamps.

Executing and Inspecting Migrations

Once our migration file is ready, we will apply all outstanding migrations to the database. From here, we run:

```
php artisan migrate
```

To confirm the current state of all migrations, we will then run the status command:

```
php artisan migrate:status
```

The migration status table makes it clear which migrations have been applied and which are still outstanding:

```
myapp — php artisan migrate:status — 80×24

pravindhandre@Pravins-MacBook-Air myapp % php artisan migrate:status
  Migration name .......................................... Batch / Status
  0001_01_01_000000_create_users_table ........................ [1] Ran
  0001_01_01_000001_create_cache_table ........................ [1] Ran
  0001_01_01_000002_create_jobs_table ......................... [1] Ran
  2026_05_09_053657_create_personal_access_tokens_table ....... [2] Ran
  2026_05_09_055030_add_two_factor_columns_to_users_table ..... [3] Ran
  2026_05_09_055149_create_posts_table ........................ [4] Ran
  2026_05_09_055545_create_comments_table ..................... [5] Ran
  2026_05_09_055704_create_tags_table ......................... [5] Ran
  2026_05_09_055709_create_post_tag_table ..................... [5] Ran

pravindhandre@Pravins-MacBook-Air myapp %
```

Fig 4.3: Migration Status

The terminal will display a table listing every migration file alongside its current status, showing **`Ran`** for applied migrations and **`Pending`** for any that have not yet been executed. It gives us a reliable snapshot of our database schema state at any point during development.

Recipe 3: Data Seeding for Consistent Testing Scenarios

A consistent and realistic dataset is invaluable for testing new features and ensuring that **`myapp`** behaves as expected under real-world conditions. During a code review session, our team agreed that simulating production-like data early in the development cycle helps surface potential issues before they reach a live environment. In this recipe, we will write a seeder class to populate the **`posts`** table with sample data, register it in the central **`DatabaseSeeder`**, and execute it using Artisan.

Creating and Writing Seeder

We then generate a new seeder class:

```
php artisan make:seeder PostsTableSeeder
```

The seeders run in order, each populating its table with sample data ready for local development:

```
myapp — php artisan db:seed --class=PostSeeder — 80×24

pravindhandre@Pravins-MacBook-Air myapp % php artisan db:seed --class=PostSeeder
 INFO  Seeding: Database\Seeders\PostSeeder
 INFO  Seeded:  Database\Seeders\PostSeeder (1.23ms)
pravindhandre@Pravins-MacBook-Air myapp %
```

Fig 4.4: Database Seeded

This creates **database/seeders/PostsTableSeeder.php**. We will then open that file and update the **run** method with the following logic:

```
<?php

namespace Database\Seeders;

use Illuminate\Database\Seeder;
use Illuminate\Support\Facades\DB;
use Carbon\Carbon;

class PostsTableSeeder extends Seeder
{
    public function run(): void
    {
        DB::table('posts')->insert([
            [
                'title'      => 'First Post',
                'content'    => 'This is the content of the first
post.',
                'user_id'    => 1,
                'created_at' => Carbon::now(),
                'updated_at' => Carbon::now(),
            ],
            [
```

```
                    'title'        => 'Second Post',
                    'content'      => 'Here is some content for the second
post.',
                    'user_id'      => 1,
                    'created_at' => Carbon::now(),
                    'updated_at' => Carbon::now(),
                ],
            ]);
    }
}
```

Registering and Executing Seeders

We will now open **database/seeders/DatabaseSeeder.php** and register our new seeder inside the **run** method as shown below:

```
public function run(): void
{
    $this->call([
        PostsTableSeeder::class,
    ]);
}
```

Finally, we now execute all registered seeders:

```
php artisan db:seed
```

We can verify the inserted data by connecting to the database using the MySQL client and running **SELECT * FROM posts;** to confirm the records are present.

Recipe 4: Optimizing Complex Database Queries

As **myapp** accumulates more data, we notice performance degradation when retrieving posts together with their comments. The root cause is the N+1 query problem, which occurs when we fetch all posts in one query and then fire a separate query per post to retrieve its associated comments. In a project with hundreds of posts, this pattern generates hundreds of unnecessary database round trips. We will now resolve this using Laravel's eager loading feature and verify the improvement with the Laravel Debugbar we installed in Chapter 1.

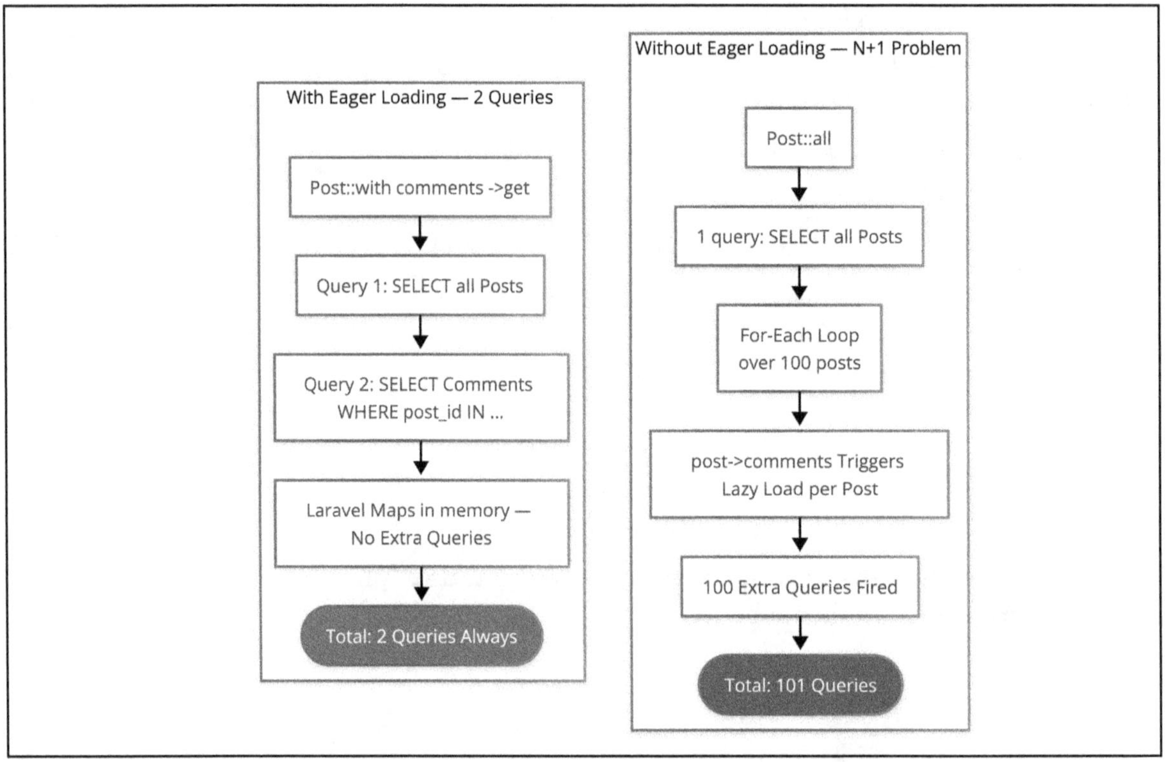

Fig4.5: N+1 Query Problem and Eager Loading Fix

The above side-by-side flowchart makes the performance difference between lazy loading and eager loading immediately visible. It is a very useful reference before applying **`with()`** in your own queries.

Identifying N+1 Query Problem

The following code illustrates the problematic pattern. We now examine what an unoptimized query loop looks like:

```
$posts = App\Models\Post::all();


foreach ($posts as $post) {
    $comments = $post->comments; // Fires a new query on every
iteration
}
```

This results in one query to fetch all posts and one additional query per post to load its comments, meaning the total query count grows linearly with the size of the dataset.

Implementing Eager Loading

To resolve this, we will update our controller method to eager load the **comments** relationship upfront. Here, we replace the unoptimized query:

```
$posts = App\Models\Post::with('comments')->get();
```

This single **with('comments')** call instructs Eloquent to fetch all posts and all their associated comments in exactly two queries, regardless of how many posts exist. Laravel handles the relationship mapping internally, so the data is available through the same **$post->comments** property without any change to the view layer. We can also eager load multiple relationships or nested relationships using an array, for example **Post::with(['comments', 'tags'])->get()**, following the same pattern as the project grows.

Verifying with Laravel Debugbar

With Laravel Debugbar active from our Chapter 1 setup, we will start the server with **php artisan serve** and navigate to the page that displays posts and comments. The Debugbar panel at the bottom of the screen will now show exactly two database queries for the page regardless of the number of posts. It confirms that the N+1 problem has been fully resolved.

Recipe 5: Building Dynamic Test Data with Model Factories

While the seeder we built in Recipe 3 works well for a small fixed dataset, manually writing insertion arrays does not scale when we need hundreds of records with varied, realistic data. Laravel's model factory system, powered by the Faker library, allows us to define templates for generating dynamic test data programmatically. In this recipe, we will define factories for our **Post** and **Comment** models, use them inside our seeders to generate large volumes of realistic records, and confirm the results in our database.

Creating Post and Comment Factories

Next, we generate factories for both models:

```
php artisan make:factory PostFactory --model=Post
php artisan make:factory CommentFactory --model=Comment
```

These commands create factory files in the **database/factories** directory. We will then open **database/factories/PostFactory.php** and define the **definition** method as follows:

```
<?php
```

```
namespace Database\Factories;

use App\Models\User;
use Illuminate\Database\Eloquent\Factories\Factory;

class PostFactory extends Factory
{
    public function definition(): array
    {
        return [
            'title'   => fake()->sentence(6),
            'content' => fake()->paragraphs(3, true),
            'user_id' => User::factory(),
        ];
    }
}
```

Next, we will open **database/factories/CommentFactory.php** and define its template:

```
<?php

namespace Database\Factories;

use App\Models\Post;
use Illuminate\Database\Eloquent\Factories\Factory;

class CommentFactory extends Factory
{
    public function definition(): array
    {
        return [
            'post_id' => Post::factory(),
```

```
            'author'   => fake()->name(),
            'content'  => fake()->paragraph(2, true),
        ];
    }
}
```

The **fake()** helper provides access to Faker's full library of data generators, including **sentence()**, **paragraphs()**, **name()**, and **paragraph()**. Passing **User::factory()** and **Post::factory()** as values for the foreign key columns tells Laravel to automatically create the parent record if one does not already exist, making factories fully self-contained and composable. We will also need to ensure the **Post** and **Comment** models use the **HasFactory** trait by verifying the following is present in each model class:

```
use Illuminate\Database\Eloquent\Factories\HasFactory;

class Post extends Model
{
    use HasFactory;
    // ...
}
```

Using Factories inside Seeders

We will now update **DatabaseSeeder.php** to use our new factories for generating a richer dataset. At this point, we replace the previous seeder logic:

```
public function run(): void
{
    \App\Models\Post::factory()
        ->count(50)
        ->has(\App\Models\Comment::factory()->count(5))
        ->create();
}
```

This creates fifty posts, each with five associated comments, all using Faker-generated data. The **has()** method is Eloquent's factory relationship helper, which handles the foreign key wiring automatically. We will then execute the seeders:

```
php artisan db:seed
```

The terminal will confirm successful seeding, and we can connect to our database to verify that fifty posts and two hundred and fifty comments have been inserted with varied, realistic content across all records.

Recipe 6: Writing Reusable Query Logic with Eloquent Scopes

As **myapp** grows, we will find ourselves repeating the same query constraints in multiple controllers and service classes. For example, we might need to filter posts by their published status or retrieve only the posts belonging to the currently authenticated user in several different places. Duplicating these constraints leads to inconsistencies and makes future changes error-prone. Eloquent local scopes solve this by encapsulating reusable query logic directly in the model, giving us clean, expressive, chainable methods that can be composed together wherever we need them.

Defining Local Scopes on Post Model

We will need to add a **published** boolean column to the **posts** table before defining our scopes. We can now generate a new migration:

```
php artisan make:migration add_published_to_posts_table --table=posts
```

We will then open the generated migration file and update it as follows:

```
public function up(): void
{
    Schema::table('posts', function (Blueprint $table) {
        $table->boolean('published')->default(false)->after('content');
    });
}

public function down(): void
{
    Schema::table('posts', function (Blueprint $table) {
        $table->dropColumn('published');
    });
```

```
}
```

After running **php artisan migrate**, we will open **app/Models/Post.php** and define two local scopes. From here, we add the following methods to the model:

```
/**
 * Scope a query to only include published posts.
 */
public function scopePublished($query)
{
    return $query->where('published', true);
}

/**
 * Scope a query to only include posts belonging to a given user.
 */
public function scopeByUser($query, int $userId)
{
    return $query->where('user_id', $userId);
}
```

Local scope methods follow the **scope** prefix naming convention. Laravel automatically strips that prefix when we call the scope, so **scopePublished** becomes **published()** and **scopeByUser** becomes **byUser()** at the call site.

Using Scopes in Controllers

We will now use our new scopes inside a controller method. So here, we will then open **PostController.php** and update the **index** method as follows:

```
public function index()
{
    $posts = Post::published()
        ->byUser(auth()->id())
        ->with(['comments', 'tags'])
        ->latest()
```

```
        ->get();

    return view('posts.index', compact('posts'));
}
```

This single fluent query chain retrieves only published posts belonging to the authenticated user, eager loads their comments and tags to avoid the N+1 problem we resolved in Recipe 4, and orders results by the most recent first. Each scope we defined in the model is now reusable across every controller, service, or command in **myapp** without duplicating the underlying **where** conditions. Adding a new filtering requirement in the future means updating one scope method rather than hunting through every location where the constraint is applied.

Summary

Throughout this chapter, we built out the complete data layer of **myapp** using a structured and incremental approach. We started by defining Eloquent models for **Post**, **Tag**, and **Comment**, establishing one-to-many relationships between users, posts, and comments, and a many-to-many relationship between posts and tags backed by a pivot table. We then created and executed migration files to version-control our schema changes, including the **comments** table and the **post_tag** pivot table, using Artisan throughout.

We populated our database at first, through a manual seeder class with fixed records, and then through model factories with Faker-generated data, creating fifty posts with five comments each in a single composable command. We resolved the N+1 query problem by applying eager loading with **with()**, confirmed the improvement using Laravel Debugbar, and extended our query optimization practices by defining local scopes on the **Post** model to encapsulate reusable filtering logic. Every recipe in this chapter builds on the same project and prepares the data layer for the more advanced features we will introduce in the chapters ahead.

CHAPTER 5

DATA VALIDATION AND ERROR MANAGEMENT

Overview

In this chapter, we will build a solid foundation for data validation and error management in **myapp**. We will implement server-side validation using Laravel's built-in **Validator** to enforce business rules on every incoming request. We will then extend that with custom validation rules and tailored error messages that communicate precise issues to the user.

We will also centralize exception handling using Laravel 12's **bootstrap/app.php** approach, ensuring that all errors are captured, logged, and rendered consistently whether the request comes from a browser or an API client. Finally, we will integrate Laravel Pulse for real-time error monitoring, giving our team a live dashboard that surfaces issues as they occur in production. Each recipe builds directly on the **myapp** infrastructure established in the previous chapters.

Recipe 1: Implementing Server-Side Data Validation

After reviewing **myapp** in a team meeting, we identify that inconsistencies and potential security vulnerabilities could arise without proper validation of user inputs. Fields like email addresses, passwords, and usernames must conform to specific formats and rules before we allow them near our database. In this recipe, we will build a robust validation layer using Laravel's Form Request class, which centralizes all validation rules in a dedicated file and keeps our controllers clean and focused on business logic alone.

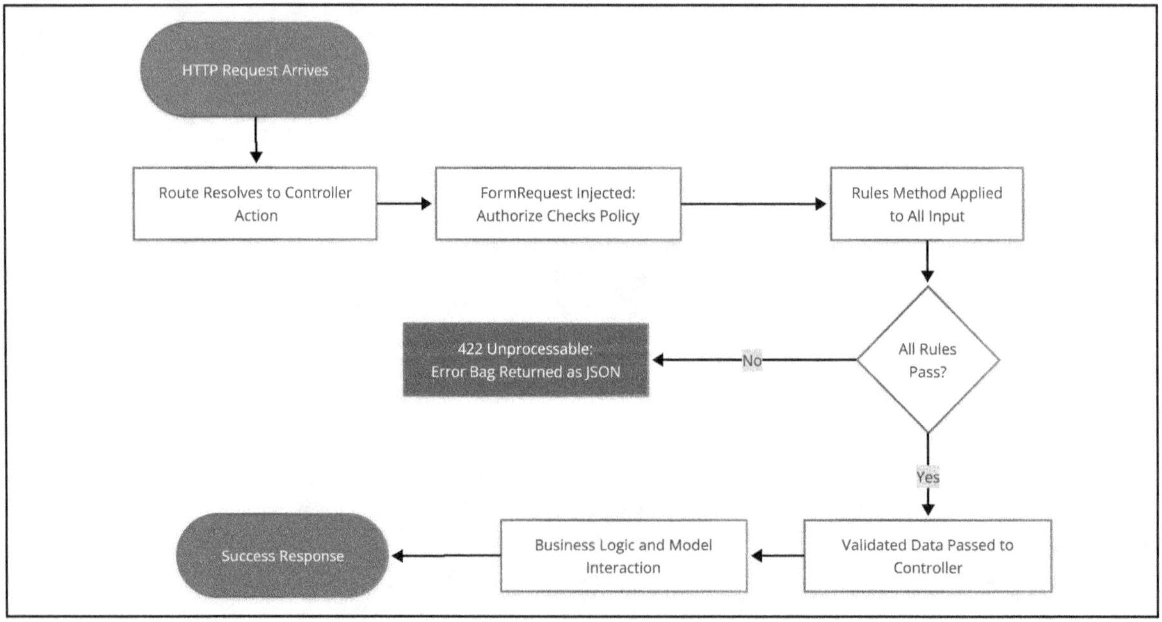

Fig 5.1: Form Request Validation Lifecycle

The flowchart above traces a request from its arrival at the route through the FormRequest gate, showing both the clean success path and the 422 error branch back to the client.

Generating Form Request Class

Laravel's Form Request class provides a clean, testable home for our validation rules, keeping them out of the controller entirely. We then generate the dedicated class:

```
php artisan make:request RegisterUserRequest
```

This creates a new file at **app/Http/Requests/RegisterUserRequest.php**. We will now open it and inspect **authorize()** and **rules()**. These two methods together define both who can submit the request and what the submitted data must look like. The **authorize()** method returns **true** by default, meaning any authenticated user may proceed through the request.

Defining Validation Rules

With the class generated, we will now populate the **rules()** method with the field-level constraints appropriate for our registration form. We now define the rules as follows:

```
public function rules(): array
{
    return [
        'name'     => ['required', 'string', 'max:100'],
        'email'    => ['required', 'email', 'unique:users,email'],
        'password' => ['required', 'string', 'min:8', 'confirmed'],
    ];
}
```

The **unique:users,email** rule queries the **users** table to confirm that the email address has not already been registered. The **confirmed** rule on **password** requires a matching **password_confirmation** field in the payload. Laravel evaluates these rules in order and stops at the first failure for each field, returning only the errors that are actionable by the user.

Defining Custom Error Messages

While Laravel generates default error messages for all built-in rules, we can tailor these messages to match the voice and tone of our application. So here, we will then override the **messages()** method inside **RegisterUserRequest** with the following definitions:

```
public function messages(): array
{
```

```
    return [
        'name.required'       => 'Please enter your full name.',
        'email.unique'        => 'This email address is already registered.',
        'password.confirmed' => 'The password confirmation does not match.',
        'password.min'        => 'Your password must be at least 8 characters long.',
    ];
}
```

These custom strings replace Laravel's generic phrasing with clear, user-friendly feedback. When validation fails, the **$errors** bag in our Blade views surfaces these strings directly against the relevant fields, giving users specific guidance rather than technical rule names they would not recognize.

Applying Form Request in Controller

The final step is wiring the Form Request class into our controller. Here, we open the registration controller and type-hint the request class in the method signature as shown below:

```
use App\Http\Requests\RegisterUserRequest;


public function register(RegisterUserRequest $request): RedirectResponse
{
    $data = $request->validated();


    User::create([
        'name'     => $data['name'],
        'email'    => $data['email'],
        'password' => bcrypt($data['password']),
    ]);


    return redirect()->route('dashboard');
}
```

At this point, the Form Request intercepts incoming data before the method body runs. If validation fails, Laravel automatically redirects the user back with error messages populated in the session. The **$request->validated()** call returns only the fields that passed all their rules, giving us a clean, safe array to pass directly into the model.

Recipe 2: Custom Validation Rules and Feedback

As **myapp** matures, we encounter scenarios where built-in validation rules are not sufficient. Our team identifies that usernames must not contain prohibited words such as **admin** or **root**, which no standard Laravel rule covers. We also want to provide targeted, human-readable error messages rather than generic ones so that users understand exactly what they need to correct. In this recipe, we will create a reusable custom Rule class, implement our validation logic inside it, attach it to the Form Request we built in Recipe 1, and confirm the rule behaves correctly before moving on.

Generating Custom Rule Class

Laravel provides a dedicated Artisan command for scaffolding custom Rule objects. So here, we will generate the class:

```
php artisan make:rule NoBannedWords
```

This creates a new file at **app/Rules/NoBannedWords.php**. We will now open this file and note the single **validate()** method that Laravel expects us to implement. This method receives the attribute name, the submitted value, and a **$fail** callable that we invoke whenever the rule is not satisfied. The rule class is intentionally minimal, making it straightforward to unit-test in isolation.

Implementing Validation Logic

With the class in place, we will now write the logic that checks whether the submitted value contains any disallowed terms. So here, we will then populate the **validate()** method as shown below:

```
namespace App\Rules;


use Closure;

use Illuminate\Contracts\Validation\ValidationRule;


class NoBannedWords implements ValidationRule

{
```

```
    protected array $banned = ['spam', 'admin', 'root'];

    public function validate(string $attribute, mixed $value, Closure
$fail): void
    {
        foreach ($this->banned as $word) {
            if (str_contains(strtolower($value), $word)) {
                $fail("The :attribute contains a reserved word that is
not permitted.");
                return;
            }
        }
    }
}
```

The loop compares the submitted value against each entry in the **$banned** array using a case-insensitive check. As soon as a match is found, we invoke **$fail** with a descriptive message and return immediately to avoid redundant iterations. The **:attribute** placeholder is automatically replaced by Laravel with the actual field name when the message is rendered in the view.

Attaching Rule to Form Request

Now we will integrate the custom rule into the **RegisterUserRequest** class we built in Recipe 1. So here, we will then update the **rules()** method to include the new rule on the **name** field as shown below:

```
use App\Rules\NoBannedWords;

public function rules(): array
{
    return [
        'name'     => ['required', 'string', 'max:100', new
NoBannedWords],
        'email'    => ['required', 'email', 'unique:users,email'],
        'password' => ['required', 'string', 'min:8', 'confirmed'],
    ];
```

```
}
```

We instantiate the rule class and include it alongside the built-in rules in the same array. Laravel evaluates each rule in order, and if **NoBannedWords** triggers a failure, the remaining rules for that field are not evaluated. The error message surfaces in the **$errors** bag alongside any other validation failures on the form, with no additional wiring required in the controller.

Verifying Rule in Browser

At this point, the custom rule is fully wired and we can confirm it works before moving on. At this point, we start the development server:

```
php artisan serve
```

Once the server is running at **http://127.0.0.1:8000**, we can open the registration form and submit a username containing a banned term such as "adminuser". The form should re-render with our custom validation error displayed beneath the name field. It helps us to confirm that the rule is active and correctly intercepting disallowed input before it reaches the controller.

Recipe 3: Centralized Exception Handling

Even with rigorous validation in place, unexpected exceptions will surface under real traffic conditions. We need to ensure that when they do, every error is captured, logged, and returned to the client in a consistent format. In Laravel 12, the preferred approach for centralizing exception handling is the **->withExceptions()** callback in **bootstrap/app.php**, which aligns with the same bootstrap-first pattern we used for middleware registration in Chapter 3. This replaces the need to modify **app/Exceptions/Handler.php** directly and keeps all application-level configuration consolidated in one file.

The following pipeline shows Laravel's centralized handler evaluating every thrown exception and routes it to a custom renderer, a named HTTP error view, or a generic 500 fallback:

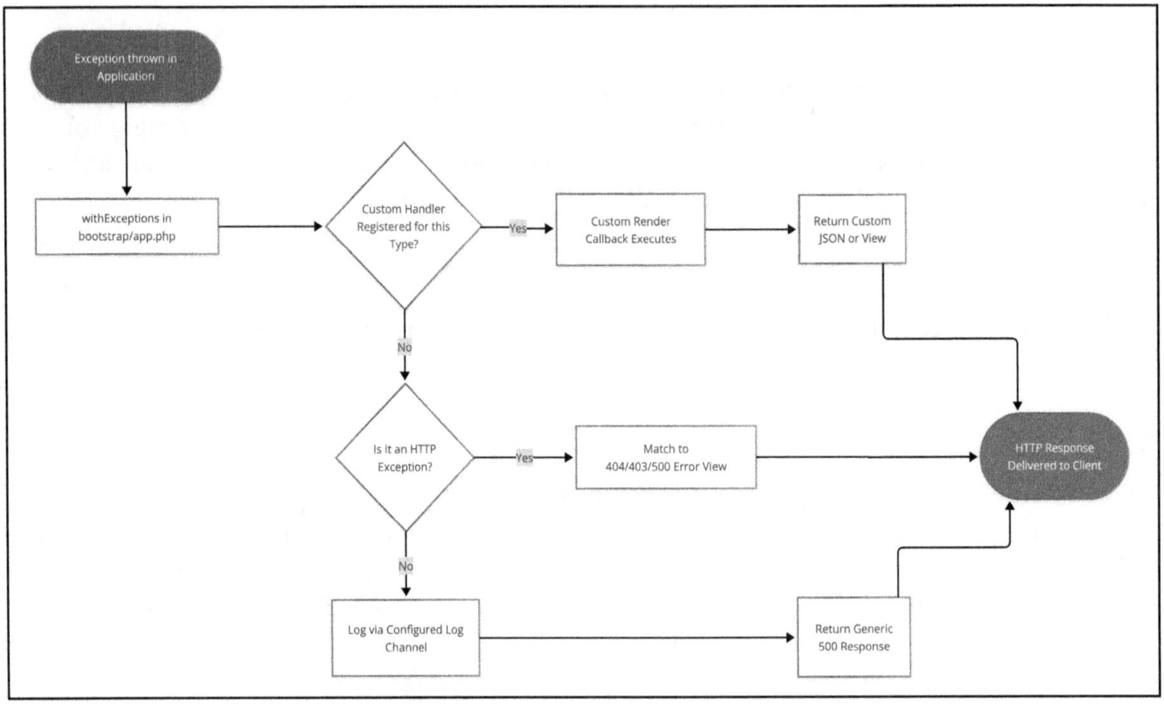

Fig 5.2: Exception Handler Decision Pipeline

Configuring Report and Render

So here, we will then open **bootstrap/app.php** and update the exception configuration as follows:

```
use Illuminate\Foundation\Application;
use Illuminate\Foundation\Configuration\Exceptions;
use Illuminate\Http\Request;

return Application::configure(basePath: dirname(__DIR__))
    ->withRouting(
        web: __DIR__.'/../routes/web.php',
        api: __DIR__.'/../routes/api.php',
        commands: __DIR__.'/../routes/console.php',
    )
    ->withMiddleware(function ($middleware) {
        $middleware->alias([
```

```
        'role' => \App\Http\Middleware\RoleMiddleware::class,
    ]);
})
->withExceptions(function (Exceptions $exceptions) {

    $exceptions->report(function (Throwable $e) {
        \Illuminate\Support\Facades\Log::error(
            'Exception: ' . $e->getMessage(),
            ['exception' => $e]
        );
    });

    $exceptions->render(function (Throwable $e, Request $request) {
        if ($request->wantsJson()) {
            return response()->json([
                'success' => false,
                'message' => 'An error occurred.',
                'error'   => $e->getMessage(),
            ], 500);
        }
    });

})->create();
```

The **report** callback fires whenever an exception needs to be logged. We use Laravel's **Log** facade to write the message and full exception context to our application log. The **render** callback intercepts every exception before it reaches the client. When the incoming request expects JSON, it returns a consistent envelope with a **success** flag, a human-readable message, and the exception detail. For standard browser requests, returning **null** from the callback falls through to Laravel's default error page rendering, so we do not need to replicate that logic ourselves.

Testing Handler

To confirm that our configuration is working, we will temporarily throw an exception inside a controller method. We can now add the following line to any controller action:

```
throw new \Exception('Testing centralized exception handling.');
```

After visiting the associated route via the browser and again via Postman, we should see Laravel's default error page for the browser request and a structured JSON response for the API request. Once verified, we will remove the test line before continuing.

Recipe 4: Monitoring Application Errors with Laravel Pulse

After deploying **myapp**, our team notices intermittent errors that are difficult to diagnose from log files alone. We need a real-time dashboard that aggregates error events, performance metrics, and system health indicators in a single view. Laravel Pulse is purpose-built for this, and it integrates directly with Laravel's logging infrastructure without requiring a third-party service. In this recipe, we will install Pulse, configure a dedicated logging channel, emit a custom error event from a controller, and set up a critical alert to notify the team proactively.

Installing and Publishing Laravel Pulse

So here, we will first add Pulse to **myapp**:

```
composer require laravel/pulse
```

Once installed, we will publish the Pulse configuration and frontend assets:

```
php artisan vendor:publish --
provider="Laravel\Pulse\PulseServiceProvider"
```

Next, we will run the migrations that Pulse requires for its data tables:

```
php artisan migrate
```

Configuring Logging Channel

We will now add a dedicated logging channel for Pulse in **config/logging.php**. So here, we will then add the following entry to the **channels** array:

```
'pulse' => [
    'driver' => 'daily',
    'path'   => storage_path('logs/pulse.log'),
    'level'  => 'error',
    'days'   => 14,
```

```
],
```

Then, we will update the **.env** file to route error-level logs to this channel:

```
LOG_CHANNEL=pulse
```

Emitting Custom Errors and Setting Alerts

We will now log a structured error event from a controller action to demonstrate Pulse capturing application-specific context. From here, we update any controller method as follows:

```
use Illuminate\Support\Facades\Log;

public function processData()
{
    try {
        throw new \Exception('Simulated critical failure in
processData.');
    } catch (\Exception $e) {
        Log::channel('pulse')->error('Critical error in processData', [
            'error'   => $e->getMessage(),
            'user_id' => auth()->id(),
            'action'  => 'processData',
        ]);
    }
}
```

To enable proactive alerting, we will then open **config/pulse.php** and add the following alerts configuration:

```
'alerts' => [
    'critical' => [
        'enabled'  => true,
        'channels' => ['mail', 'slack'],
        'mail'     => [
            'to'      => 'devteam@example.com',
            'subject' => 'Critical Error in myapp',
```

```
        ],
        'slack' => [
            'webhook_url' => env('SLACK_WEBHOOK_URL'),
        ],
    ],
],
```

With this in place, we can start the server with **`php artisan serve`** and navigate to **`http://127.0.0.1:8000/pulse`** to access the Pulse dashboard.

Fig 5.3: Laravel Dashboard - Pulse

Any logged error will appear there in real time, and any event tagged as **`critical`** will trigger the configured mail and Slack notifications. In parallel, we can use Laravel Debugbar to cross-reference the query count and performance metrics on the same page load, giving us a complete picture of the application's health from two complementary tools.

Summary

Throughout this chapter, we built a layered approach to data integrity and error visibility in

myapp. We started by implementing server-side validation using Laravel's **Validator**, enforcing field-level rules on name, email, and password inputs in the registration flow. We then extended that foundation with closure-based custom validation rules and a tailored messages array, giving users precise, actionable feedback when their inputs fall outside our business constraints.

We centralized exception handling using Laravel 12's **->withExceptions()** callback in **bootstrap/app.php**, logging all errors through the **report** callback and returning consistent JSON responses for API clients through the **render** callback. Finally, we integrated Laravel Pulse to bring real-time error visibility to the team, configuring a dedicated log channel, emitting structured error events from a controller, and setting up critical alerts over both email and Slack. Every step in this chapter strengthens a different layer of **myapp**'s resilience and observability.

CHAPTER 6

ALERTS, NOTIFICATIONS, AND PERFORMANCE MONITORING

Overview

In this chapter, we will improve **myapp**'s responsiveness and user engagement by building a layered system for alerts, notifications, and performance monitoring. We will set up in-app alerts using Laravel's database notification channel so that users receive real-time feedback directly inside the application. We will then configure multi-channel notifications to deliver important updates over email and SMS using Laravel's native mail driver and the Vonage SMS integration.

Further, we will integrate real-time push notifications using Laravel Broadcasting with Pusher and Laravel Echo, enabling instant message delivery to connected browser clients without a page refresh. We will close the chapter by using Laravel Telescope and Debugbar to monitor key application metrics including execution times, memory usage, and query efficiency, complemented by Linux system-level tools for a complete performance picture.

Recipe 1: Deploying Real-time In-app Alerts

As **myapp** grows, users begin missing important updates because the application has no mechanism to surface them proactively. In a recent team meeting, we identify that critical events such as system warnings, new messages, and promotional notifications need to reach the user inside the application the moment they occur. We will use Laravel's Notification system with the database channel to store and display these alerts. This approach keeps notifications persistent in the database so that users see them even if they were not online when the event was triggered.

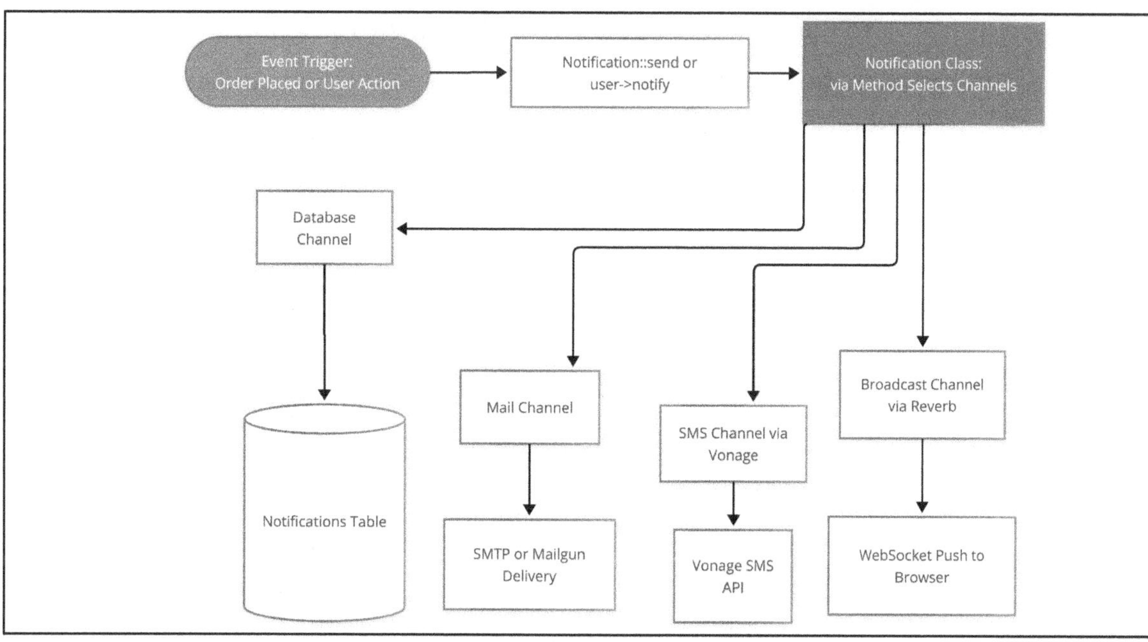

Fig 6.1: Notification Channel Architecture

The above fan-out diagram shows a single notification class simultaneously delivers alerts across multiple independent channels through Laravel's unified notification system.

Enabling Notifications Table

The **`User`** model in **`myapp`** already uses the **`Notifiable`** trait from our Laravel Breeze setup in Chapter 3. Before sending database notifications, we need the supporting table. We then create and run the notifications migration:

```
php artisan notifications:table
php artisan migrate
```

The database notifications table is created, enabling Laravel to persist notifications rather than send them in-memory:

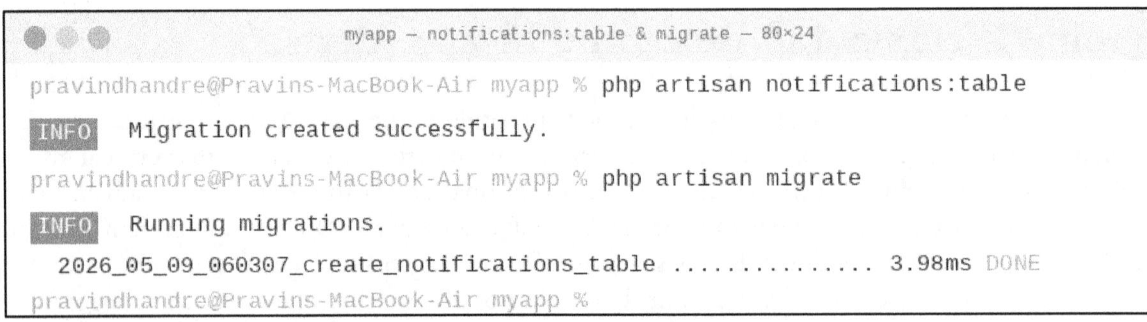

Fig 6.2: Notifications Table Migrated

This creates a **`notifications`** table that Laravel uses to store all database-channel notification records.

Creating Alert Notification Class

We now generate a custom notification class:

```
php artisan make:notification UserAlertNotification
```

We will then open **`app/Notifications/UserAlertNotification.php`** and update it as follows:

```
<?php

namespace App\Notifications;

use Illuminate\Bus\Queueable;
```

```php
use Illuminate\Notifications\Notification;

class UserAlertNotification extends Notification
{
    use Queueable;

    public function __construct(
        protected string $alertMessage,
        protected string $alertType = 'info'
    ) {}

    public function via($notifiable): array
    {
        return ['database'];
    }

    public function toDatabase($notifiable): array
    {
        return [
            'message'   => $this->alertMessage,
            'type'      => $this->alertType,
            'timestamp' => now()->toDateTimeString(),
        ];
    }
}
```

The **via()** method returns **['database']**, directing Laravel to persist the notification payload returned by **toDatabase()**. The **type** field accepts values like **info**, **warning**, or **error**, which we can map to CSS classes in the view for visual differentiation.

Sending and Displaying Alerts

We will now trigger the notification from **DashboardController**. So here, we will then update the **show** method as follows:

```
public function show()
{
    $user = auth()->user();
    $user->notify(new UserAlertNotification('You have a new system
update available!', 'info'));
    return view('dashboard');
}
```

To display notifications in the UI, we will then add the following block to **resources/views/layouts/app.blade.php**:

```
<div class="notifications">
    @foreach (auth()->user()->unreadNotifications as $notification)
        <div class="alert alert-{{ $notification->data['type'] }}">
            {{ $notification->data['message'] }}
            <small>{{ $notification->data['timestamp'] }}</small>
        </div>
    @endforeach
</div>
```

To allow users to clear their alerts, we will then add a route and controller method as follows:

```
// routes/web.php
Route::get('/notifications/mark-as-read',
[NotificationController::class, 'markAsRead'])
    ->name('notifications.markAsRead')->middleware('auth');

// app/Http/Controllers/NotificationController.php
public function markAsRead()
{
    auth()->user()->unreadNotifications->markAsRead();
    return redirect()->back();
}
```

With the notification dispatched, Laravel will now insert a new record into the **notifications** table, storing the channel type, the notifiable model identifier, and the serialized data payload. We will then be able to retrieve all unread notifications for a user through **$user->unreadNotifications** or mark them as read via **$user->markAsRead()**. At this point, our database notification pipeline is fully functional, and it integrates cleanly with any front-end polling or real-time broadcasting layer we add later in this chapter.

Recipe 2: Configuring Email and SMS Notifications

Our team agrees that critical events such as account security warnings and transactional alerts must reach users outside the application as well. In this recipe, we will build a notification class that delivers updates over both email and SMS. For SMS delivery in Laravel 12, we use the Vonage channel, which supersedes the legacy Nexmo integration. The two channels share the same notification class, keeping our code consolidated and easy to maintain.

Creating Notification Class

Here, we generate the notification:

```
php artisan make:notification ImportantEventNotification
```

We will then install the Vonage notification channel package:

```
composer require laravel/vonage-notification-channel
```

The Vonage notification channel registers alongside the underlying SDK that handles SMS delivery:

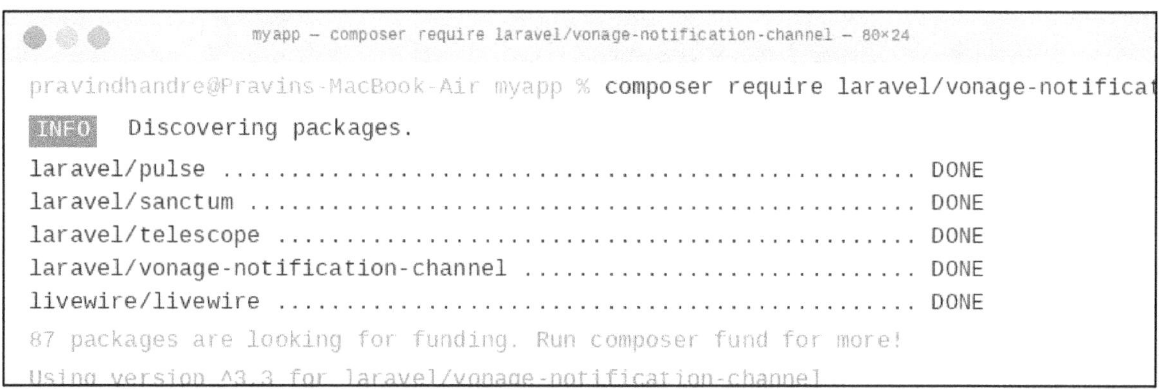

Fig 6.3: Vonage Channel Installed

Next, we will open **app/Notifications/ImportantEventNotification.php** and update it as follows:

```
<?php
```

```
namespace App\Notifications;

use Illuminate\Bus\Queueable;
use Illuminate\Contracts\Queue\ShouldQueue;
use Illuminate\Notifications\Notification;
use Illuminate\Notifications\Messages\MailMessage;
use Illuminate\Notifications\Messages\VonageMessage;

class ImportantEventNotification extends Notification implements
ShouldQueue
{
    use Queueable;

    public function __construct(
        protected string $eventMessage,
        protected array  $eventDetails = []
    ) {}

    public function via($notifiable): array
    {
        return ['mail', 'vonage'];
    }

    public function toMail($notifiable): MailMessage
    {
        return (new MailMessage)
            ->subject('Important Update from myapp')
            ->greeting('Hello ' . $notifiable->name . ',')
            ->line($this->eventMessage)
            ->line('Details: ' . implode(', ', $this->eventDetails))
            ->action('View Details', url('/dashboard'))
            ->line('Thank you for using our application.');
```

```
    }

    public function toVonage($notifiable): VonageMessage
    {
        return (new VonageMessage)
            ->content('Important update: ' . $this->eventMessage);
    }
}
```

Implementing **ShouldQueue** ensures that both the email and SMS are dispatched asynchronously via the queue, preventing notification delivery from slowing down the HTTP response.

Configuring Vonage Credentials

We will then update **.env** file with the Vonage API credentials obtained from the Vonage dashboard:

```
VONAGE_KEY=your_vonage_key
VONAGE_SECRET=your_vonage_secret
VONAGE_SMS_FROM=your_sender_number
```

To dispatch this notification, we will then call it from **DashboardController** as follows:

```
public function alertUser()
{
    $user = auth()->user();
    $user->notify(new ImportantEventNotification(
        'Your account has a critical update. Please review it immediately.',
        ['Security Issue', 'Action Required']
    ));

    return redirect()->back()->with('status', 'Notification sent successfully.');
}
```

With the **VonageMessage** notification dispatched, Laravel will now route the message through our configured Vonage gateway and deliver it as an SMS to the phone number returned by the **routeNotificationForVonage()** method on our **User** model. We can verify delivery by checking the Vonage dashboard or by inspecting the outgoing message log. At this point, our SMS notification channel is fully wired into the Laravel notification system, and we can reuse this same pattern for any other event-driven text message our application needs to send.

Recipe 3: Integrating Real-time Push Notifications

With in-app and external notifications in place, users now ask for updates that appear instantly in their browser without refreshing the page. We will use Laravel Broadcasting with Pusher as the WebSocket provider and Laravel Echo on the client side to achieve this. In Laravel 12, the broadcasting is scaffolded via a dedicated Artisan command, and the Vite build tool replaces the legacy Mix setup, which means our JavaScript environment variables and import syntax have changed from earlier editions.

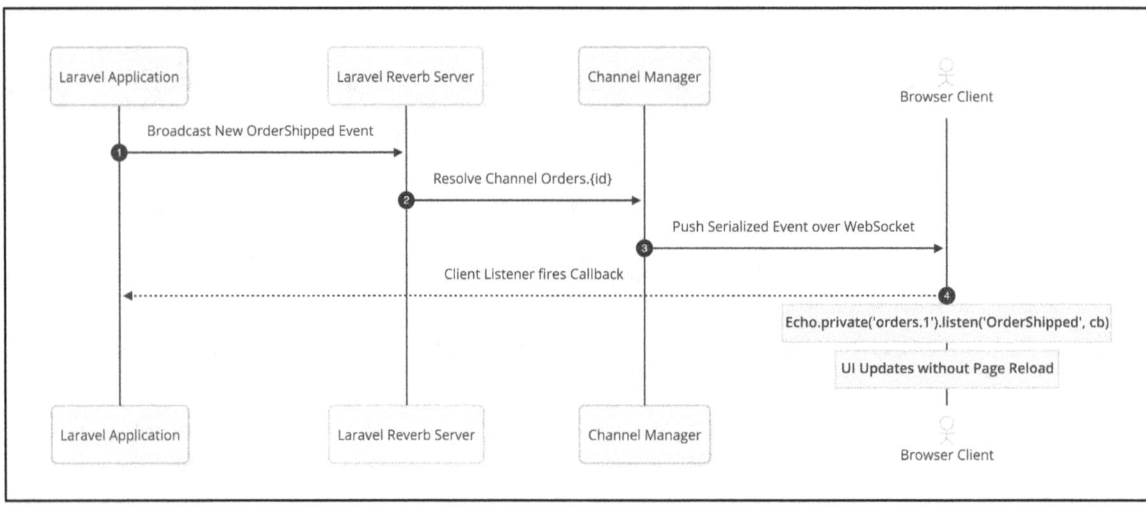

Fig 6.4: Laravel Reverb WebSocket Broadcasting

The above sequence diagram traces a broadcast event from the moment it is fired in Laravel all the way to the live UI update in the connected browser, including the channel resolution step.

Scaffolding Broadcasting Layer

Next, we scaffold the broadcasting infrastructure in Laravel 12:

```
php artisan install:broadcasting
```

It creates **config/broadcasting.php**, registers the broadcasting service provider, and scaffolds the necessary channel routes. We will then update **.env** with our Pusher credentials:

```
BROADCAST_CONNECTION=pusher
PUSHER_APP_ID=your_pusher_app_id
PUSHER_APP_KEY=your_pusher_app_key
PUSHER_APP_SECRET=your_pusher_app_secret
PUSHER_APP_CLUSTER=your_pusher_cluster

VITE_PUSHER_APP_KEY="${PUSHER_APP_KEY}"
VITE_PUSHER_APP_CLUSTER="${PUSHER_APP_CLUSTER}"
```

Note that Laravel 12 uses **BROADCAST_CONNECTION** rather than the **BROADCAST_DRIVER** key used in earlier versions. The **VITE_PUSHER_*** variables expose the credentials to our frontend via Vite's environment system.

Creating and Broadcasting Event

At this point, we generate a broadcastable event:

```
php artisan make:event NewChatMessage
```

We will then open **app/Events/NewChatMessage.php** and update it as follows:

```
<?php

namespace App\Events;

use Illuminate\Broadcasting\Channel;
use Illuminate\Queue\SerializesModels;
use Illuminate\Broadcasting\InteractsWithSockets;
use Illuminate\Contracts\Broadcasting\ShouldBroadcast;

class NewChatMessage implements ShouldBroadcast
{
    use InteractsWithSockets, SerializesModels;

    public function __construct(
        public string $message,
```

```
        public string $sender
    ) {}

    public function broadcastOn(): Channel
    {
        return new Channel('chat');
    }

    public function broadcastAs(): string
    {
        return 'new.chat.message';
    }
}
```

We will then fire this event from **`ChatController`** as follows:

```
public function sendMessage(Request $request)
{
    $message = $request->input('message');
    $sender  = auth()->user()->name;

    event(new NewChatMessage($message, $sender));

    return response()->json(['status' => 'Message sent and
broadcasted.']);
}
```

Setting up Laravel Echo with Vite

We can now install the required JavaScript packages:

```
npm install --save laravel-echo pusher-js
```

We will then open **`resources/js/bootstrap.js`** and configure Laravel Echo using Vite's environment syntax:

```
import Echo from 'laravel-echo';
```

```
import Pusher from 'pusher-js';

window.Pusher = Pusher;

window.Echo = new Echo({
    broadcaster: 'pusher',
    key:         import.meta.env.VITE_PUSHER_APP_KEY,
    cluster:     import.meta.env.VITE_PUSHER_APP_CLUSTER,
    forceTLS:    true,
});

window.Echo.channel('chat')
    .listen('.new.chat.message', (e) => {
        const el = document.createElement('div');
        el.innerHTML = `<strong>${e.sender}:</strong> ${e.message}`;
        document.getElementById('chat-messages').appendChild(el);
    });
```

The key difference from earlier Laravel versions is the use of **import.meta.env.VITE_PUSHER_APP_KEY** instead of **process.env.MIX_PUSHER_APP_KEY**. Vite exposes only variables prefixed with **VITE_** to the frontend bundle, so the **.env** entries we added earlier must use that prefix. After updating the file, we will then compile assets with **npm run dev**, and every browser connected to the **chat** channel will receive new messages in real time as they are broadcast from the server.

Recipe 4: Monitoring System Performance Metrics

After deploying **myapp**, our team notices that some requests take longer than expected and that certain database-heavy pages spike memory usage. We need to pinpoint these bottlenecks using tools already present in our environment. Laravel Telescope, which we installed in Chapter 1, provides a detailed application-level dashboard. Laravel Debugbar gives us per-request metrics in the browser toolbar. We will combine both tools and supplement them with Linux system utilities for a complete performance picture.

Using Laravel Telescope

Telescope is already installed and migrated from our Chapter 1 setup. From here, we verify it is running by starting the server and navigating to the following address:

```
http://127.0.0.1:8000/telescope
```

The Telescope dashboard surfaces HTTP requests, query execution times, exceptions, queued jobs, and mail events in a single interface.

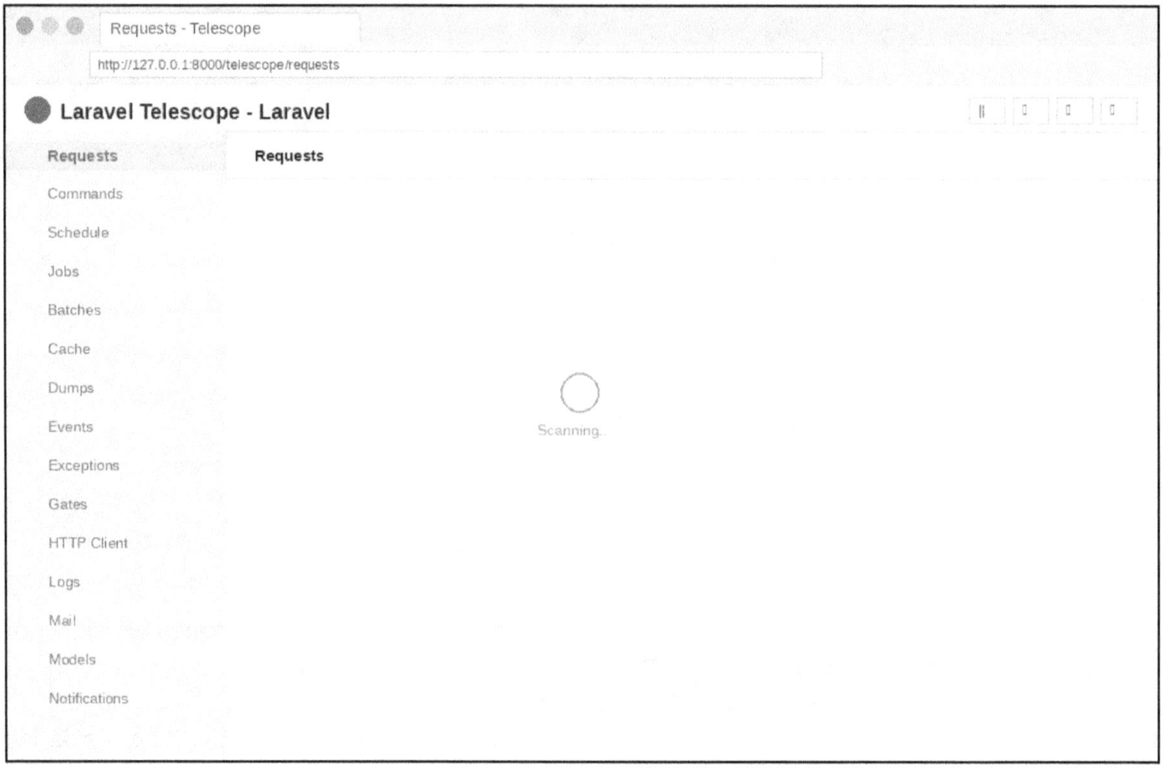

Fig 6.5: Telescope Dashboard – Requests

When we notice a slow request, we can click into it to see the full list of queries it fired, their individual durations, and the total memory consumed. This gives us a precise starting point for optimization, whether that means adding an index as covered in Chapter 4 or applying eager loading to a new relationship.

Using Laravel Debugbar

With Debugbar installed from Chapter 1, every page load in our browser displays a toolbar at the bottom of the screen showing the number of queries executed, their combined duration, memory consumption, and the route that was matched. So here, we will then navigate to the products listing page we built in Chapter 2 and observe the Debugbar panel. If the query count is higher than expected, we know an N+1 problem has been introduced and can address it using the eager loading techniques from Chapter 4.

Supplementary Linux System Metrics

While Telescope and Debugbar cover application-level metrics, we can also observe system-level resource consumption directly on our Linux server. We then open a separate terminal window and run:

```
top

htop

sudo iotop -o
```

The **top** command shows real-time CPU and memory usage across all processes. The **htop** command provides a more visual breakdown of per-core CPU load and memory consumption. The **sudo iotop -o** command displays only the processes actively performing disk read/write operations, which helps identify I/O-bound bottlenecks that application-level tools cannot surface. By comparing the Telescope request timeline against **htop** readings taken at the same moment, we can determine whether a slow request is caused by application logic, an under-indexed query, or a resource contention issue at the OS level.

Summary

Throughout this chapter, we built a complete alerting, notification, and monitoring stack for **myapp**. We started with in-app alerts using Laravel's database notification channel, storing notification payloads in the **notifications** table and rendering them in the Blade layout for logged-in users. We then extended the system to reach users outside the application by building a dual-channel notification class that delivers both email via **MailMessage** and SMS via **VonageMessage**, dispatched asynchronously through the queue.

We integrated real-time push notifications using Laravel 12's **php artisan install:broadcasting** scaffold, configured Pusher as the broadcasting driver using the updated **BROADCAST_CONNECTION** key, and built the client-side Echo listener using Vite's **import.meta.env** environment syntax. Finally, we monitored application health by combining Laravel Telescope's request and query dashboard with Debugbar's per-request toolbar, and supplemented both with **top**, **htop**, and **iotop** for system-level visibility on our Linux server.

Chapter 7

Job Queues and Background Processes

Overview

In this chapter, we will explore job queues and background processes to enhance the performance and reliability of **myapp**. We will begin by configuring queue drivers to offload heavy tasks such as sending bulk emails or generating large reports away from the main request cycle. We will then create custom job classes that encapsulate complex business logic for asynchronous processing, and implement retry strategies to manage transient failures reliably.

We will also cover automating recurring tasks using Laravel 12's updated Scheduler, which is now defined in **routes/console.php** rather than the legacy **App\Console\Kernel.php**. Finally, we will extend the chapter with two additional recipes covering job chaining for sequential workflows and job batching for parallel processing, both of which are essential patterns for production-grade background task management.

Recipe 1: Configuring Queue Drivers

Heavy tasks such as sending bulk emails, processing image uploads, or generating extensive reports should never run inside an HTTP request cycle. Each of these operations can take several seconds, directly degrading the user experience. We will offload them using Laravel's queue system, which pushes tasks onto a persistent store and processes them asynchronously via a dedicated worker process. For **myapp**, we will use the database queue driver, which stores job entries in our existing database and requires no additional infrastructure during development.

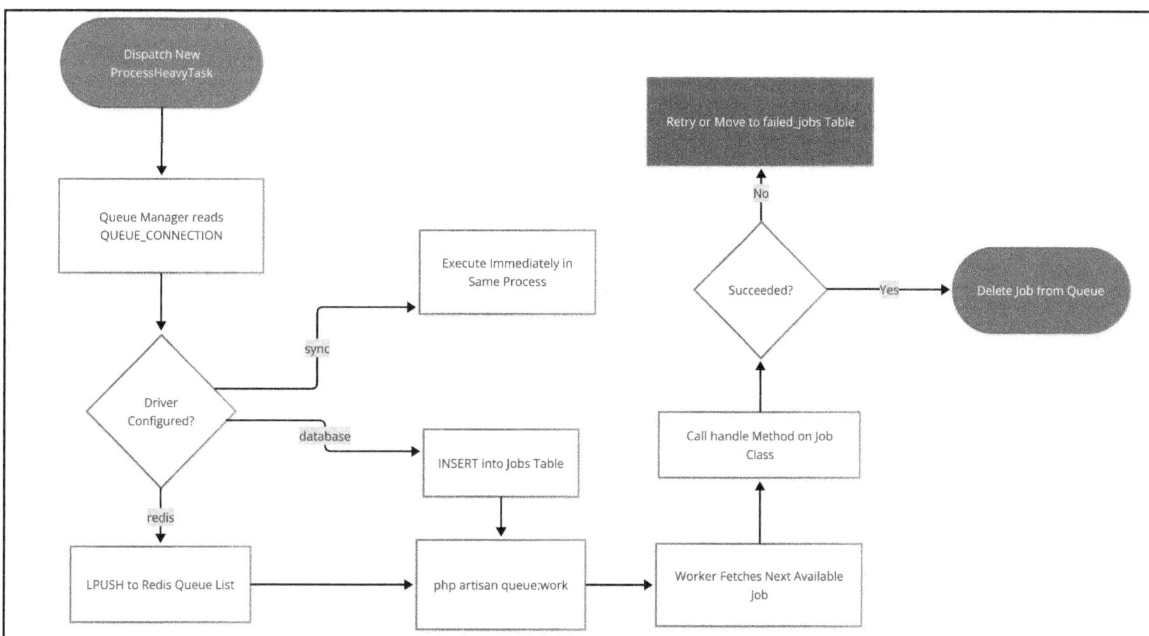

Fig 7.1: Queue Driver Architecture

The above architecture diagram shows Queue Manager routing a dispatched job to the correct driver and then the worker process picks it up for execution, including the failure path.

Setting up Queue Connection and Jobs Table

So here, we will first open the **.env** file and set the queue connection to the database driver:

```
QUEUE_CONNECTION=database
```

Next, we will generate the migration for the jobs table and apply it:

```
php artisan queue:table
php artisan migrate
```

The Laravel 12 ships all three queue migration files out of the box, and the command confirms they are already in place:

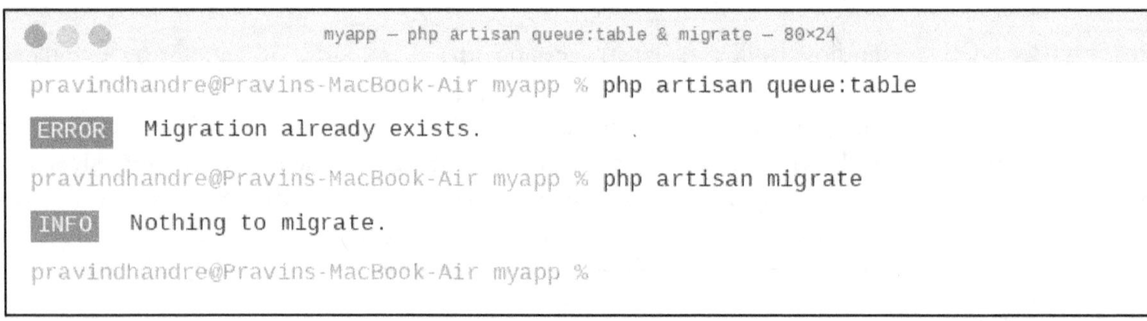

Fig 7.2: Queue Table

Creating and Dispatching Sample Job

We now generate a job class to simulate a heavy task:

```
php artisan make:job ProcessHeavyTask
```

With the queue worker running, the dispatched jobs are picked up and processed in real time as the log shows:

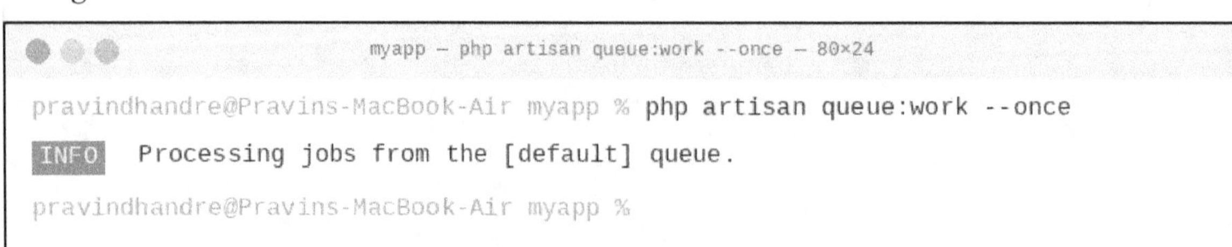

Fig 7.3: Queue Worker Running

We will then open **app/Jobs/ProcessHeavyTask.php** and update the **handle** method as follows:

```
<?php

namespace App\Jobs;

use Illuminate\Bus\Queueable;
use Illuminate\Contracts\Queue\ShouldQueue;
use Illuminate\Foundation\Bus\Dispatchable;
use Illuminate\Queue\InteractsWithQueue;
use Illuminate\Queue\SerializesModels;

class ProcessHeavyTask implements ShouldQueue
{
    use Dispatchable, InteractsWithQueue, Queueable, SerializesModels;

    public function handle(): void
    {
        sleep(10); // Simulates a long-running task
        \Log::info('ProcessHeavyTask executed successfully.');
    }
}
```

To dispatch this job from **DashboardController**, we will then add the following method:

```
public function triggerHeavyTask()
{
    ProcessHeavyTask::dispatch();
    return response()->json(['message' => 'Heavy task dispatched
successfully.']);
}
```

Running Queue Worker

So here, we will then start the queue worker from the **myapp** directory:

```
php artisan queue:work
```

The worker will pick up and process each job as it appears in the **jobs** table. For production deployments, we can use the following Supervisor configuration to keep the worker running automatically:

```
[program:laravel_queue_worker]
process_name=%(program_name)s_%(process_num)02d
command=php /path/to/myapp/artisan queue:work --sleep=3 --tries=3
autostart=true
autorestart=true
user=your_linux_user
numprocs=1
redirect_stderr=true
stdout_logfile=/path/to/myapp/storage/logs/queue.log
```

With the queue driver configured and the worker running, our application is now ready to process background jobs without delaying the HTTP response. We will now find that any class dispatched via **dispatch()** will be serialized into the queue store and picked up by the worker on its next polling cycle. At this point, the foundation for asynchronous processing is firmly in place, and we will build directly on top of this infrastructure as we create custom job classes in the next recipe.

Recipe 2: Creating Custom Job Classes

As **myapp** grows, we encounter business processes that are too complex to run within a request cycle. Report generation, for instance, involves querying large datasets, performing calculations, and persisting results, all of which can take tens of seconds. Our team agrees that encapsulating this logic in a dedicated job class is the right approach, keeping the HTTP response fast while the work continues in the background. We will build **GenerateReportJob** to demonstrate how to structure a job class that accepts input data, processes it asynchronously, and logs progress throughout.

Generating and Implementing Job

Here, we generate the job class:

```
php artisan make:job GenerateReportJob
```

We will then open **app/Jobs/GenerateReportJob.php** and update it as follows:

```
<?php

namespace App\Jobs;

use Illuminate\Bus\Queueable;
use Illuminate\Contracts\Queue\ShouldQueue;
use Illuminate\Foundation\Bus\Dispatchable;
use Illuminate\Queue\InteractsWithQueue;
use Illuminate\Queue\SerializesModels;

class GenerateReportJob implements ShouldQueue
{
    use Dispatchable, InteractsWithQueue, Queueable, SerializesModels;

    public function __construct(protected int $reportId) {}

    public function handle(): void
    {
        \Log::info("Starting report generation for report ID: {$this-
>reportId}");
        sleep(10); // Simulates processing time
        \Log::info("Completed report generation for report ID: {$this-
>reportId}");
    }
}
```

Dispatching from Controller

We will then add a dispatch method to **ReportController** as follows:

```
public function generateReport(Request $request)
{
    $reportId = $request->input('report_id', 1);
```

```
    GenerateReportJob::dispatch($reportId);

    return response()->json(['message' => 'Report generation initiated.
It will be available shortly.']);

}
```

After triggering this endpoint, we will start **`php artisan queue:work`** and watch the terminal confirm that the job was picked up and processed, and verify the log entries in **`storage/logs/laravel.log`**.

Recipe 3: Managing Job Failures

In any real-world background processing system, transient errors are inevitable. Network interruptions, temporary database connectivity issues, and third-party API timeouts can all cause a job to fail mid-execution. Without a retry strategy in place, a single transient error means permanent data loss. We will update **`GenerateReportJob`** to define retry limits and a timeout, add a **`failed()`** method for permanent failure handling, and configure the **`failed_jobs`** table so that exhausted jobs are logged and inspectable.

Configuring Retry Properties and failed() Method

So here, we will then update **`GenerateReportJob`** with the following properties and methods:

```
class GenerateReportJob implements ShouldQueue

{

    use Dispatchable, InteractsWithQueue, Queueable, SerializesModels;


    public int $tries   = 5;

    public int $timeout = 120;


    public function __construct(protected int $reportId) {}


    public function handle(): void

    {

        try {

            \Log::info("Starting report generation for ID: {$this-
>reportId}");

            sleep(10);
```

```
            if (rand(1, 3) === 1) {
                throw new \Exception("Simulated transient error.");
            }

            \Log::info("Completed report generation for ID: {$this->reportId}");
        } catch (\Exception $e) {
            \Log::error("Error in GenerateReportJob ID {$this->reportId}: " . $e->getMessage());
            throw $e; // Re-throw so Laravel retries the job
        }
    }

    public function failed(\Throwable $exception): void
    {
        \Log::critical("Job permanently failed for ID: {$this->reportId}. " . $exception->getMessage());

        // Optionally notify the admin team:
        // $admin = \App\Models\User::where('role', 'admin')->first();
        // $admin->notify(new JobFailureNotification($this->reportId, $exception->getMessage()));
    }

    public function retryUntil(): \DateTime
    {
        return now()->addHour();
    }
}
```

The **`$tries`** property caps the total number of attempts at five. The **`$timeout`** property halts any job execution that exceeds 120 seconds. Re-throwing the caught exception inside **`handle()`** signals Laravel to schedule another attempt. Once all attempts are exhausted, the framework calls **`failed()`** automatically, giving us a dedicated hook for admin alerts or cleanup logic. The

retryUntil() method provides a time-based ceiling as an alternative to a fixed attempt count.

Tracking Failed Jobs

So here, we will then create the **failed_jobs** table and run the migration:

```
php artisan queue:failed-table
php artisan migrate
```

After running the worker and triggering the job several times, we can inspect permanently failed jobs:

```
php artisan queue:failed
```

To retry a specific failed job, we will then use its ID as shown below:

```
php artisan queue:retry <id>
```

With the **failed()** method implemented and the **failed_jobs** table in place, our application will now capture every job that exceeds its retry limit and persist its payload, exception message, and timestamp for later inspection. We can review these entries at any time by running **php artisan queue:failed**, and we can replay any individual entry by passing its ID to **php artisan queue:retry**. At this point, our queue layer has a reliable safety net, and no silently discarded failures will go undetected in production.

Recipe 4: Automating Recurring Tasks with Scheduler

Recurring operations such as clearing old logs, sending weekly digests, and refreshing cached data should run automatically and reliably without manual intervention. In Laravel 12, the Scheduler is configured in **routes/console.php** using the **Schedule** facade rather than the **schedule()** method inside **App\Console\Kernel.php**, which no longer exists in a fresh installation. This change consolidates all route-like definitions into the **routes** directory and makes scheduled tasks easier to locate and manage.

Defining Scheduled Tasks

So here, we will then open **routes/console.php** and add the following schedule definitions:

```
<?php

use Illuminate\Support\Facades\Schedule;
```

```
Schedule::command('logs:clear')->daily();
Schedule::command('reports:generate')->weeklyOn(1, '8:00');
Schedule::call(function () {
    // Custom inline task logic
})->everyThirtyMinutes();
Schedule::command('reports:generate')->cron('*/5 * * * *'); // Every 5 minutes
```

Creating Custom Artisan Command

So here, we will then generate the **`logs:clear`** command:

```
php artisan make:command ClearLogs
```

We will then open **`app/Console/Commands/ClearLogs.php`** and implement the log-clearing logic:

```
<?php

namespace App\Console\Commands;

use Illuminate\Console\Command;
use Illuminate\Support\Facades\File;

class ClearLogs extends Command
{
    protected $signature   = 'logs:clear';
    protected $description = 'Clear log files from the storage/logs directory';

    public function handle(): int
    {
        $files = File::files(storage_path('logs'));

        foreach ($files as $file) {
            if ($file->getFilename() !== '.gitignore') {
```

```
                File::delete($file->getRealPath());
            }
        }

        $this->info('Logs cleared successfully.');
        return 0;
    }
}
```

We can verify the command works before scheduling it by running **`php artisan logs:clear`** directly. Once confirmed, we will then wire the Scheduler into Linux cron by editing the crontab:

```
crontab -e
```

We will then add the following single cron entry:

```
* * * * * cd /path/to/myapp && php artisan schedule:run >> /dev/null
2>&1
```

This single entry runs every minute and delegates execution timing entirely to Laravel's Scheduler, which evaluates all definitions in **`routes/console.php`** and fires only those that are due.

Recipe 5: Chaining Jobs for Sequential Workflows

Several workflows in **`myapp`** require background tasks to run in a strict sequence, where each step must complete successfully before the next one begins. A clear example is report generation followed by email dispatch, where sending the email before the report file exists would produce a broken notification. In this recipe, we will implement Laravel's job chaining using **`Bus::chain()`**, which guarantees sequential execution, halts the chain automatically on any failure, and gives us a clean place to register a catch callback for error handling.

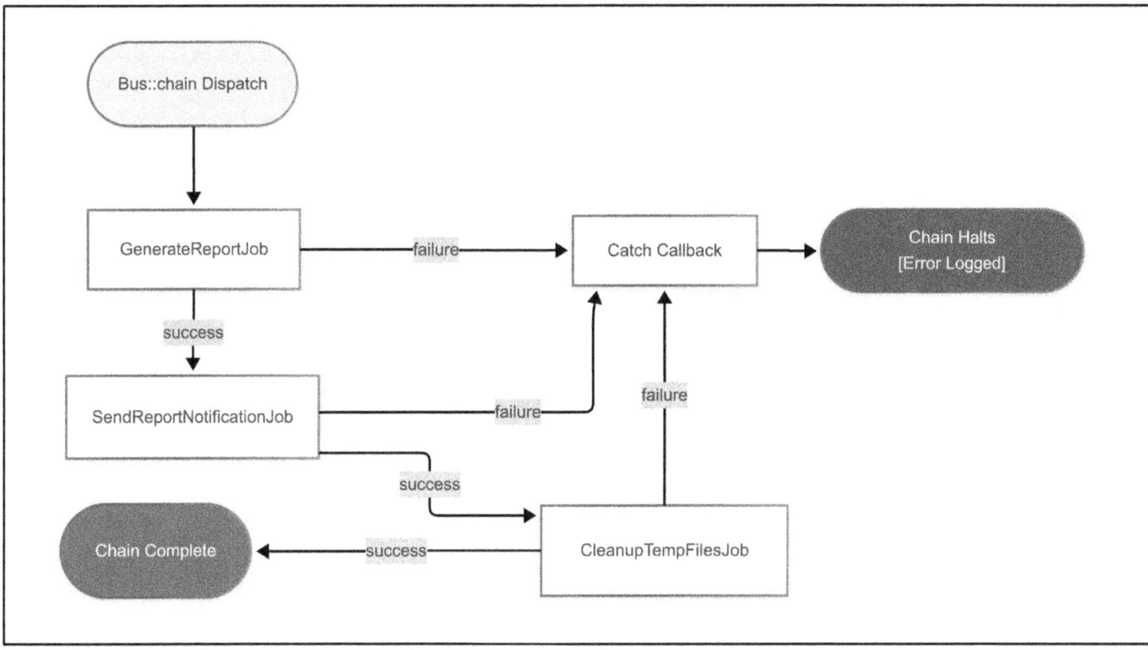

Fig 7.4: Job Chain Sequential Execution

The above flowchart describes the **Bus::chain** guaranteeing strict ordering and what happens when any job in the chain fails, including how the catch callback fires and the remaining jobs are discarded.

Defining Jobs in Chain

Before dispatching a chain, each job we intend to include must already be a fully functioning **ShouldQueue** implementation. We will build our chain around **GenerateReportJob**, which processes and saves the report file, and a new **SendReportNotificationJob**, which emails the report link to the requesting user.

So for this, we will first generate the notification job:

```
php artisan make:job SendReportNotificationJob
```

This creates a new file at **app/Jobs/SendReportNotificationJob.php**. We will now open it and implement the **handle()** method. At this point, we populate the job class as follows:

```
namespace App\Jobs;


use App\Models\User;
use Illuminate\Bus\Queueable;
```

```php
use Illuminate\Contracts\Queue\ShouldQueue;
use Illuminate\Foundation\Bus\Dispatchable;
use Illuminate\Queue\InteractsWithQueue;
use Illuminate\Queue\SerializesModels;
use Illuminate\Support\Facades\Mail;

class SendReportNotificationJob implements ShouldQueue
{
    use Dispatchable, InteractsWithQueue, Queueable, SerializesModels;

    public function __construct(
        public int    $reportId,
        public string $reportPath
    ) {}

    public function handle(): void
    {
        $user = User::findOrFail($this->reportId);
        Mail::to($user->email)->send(new
\App\Mail\ReportReadyMail($this->reportPath));
        \Log::info("Report notification sent to {$user->email}");
    }
}
```

Dispatching Chain with Bus::chain()

With both jobs ready, we will now dispatch them as an ordered chain so that **`SendReportNotificationJob`** runs only after **`GenerateReportJob`** finishes successfully. So here, we will then add the following method to our **`ReportController`**:

```php
use Illuminate\Support\Facades\Bus;
use App\Jobs\GenerateReportJob;
use App\Jobs\SendReportNotificationJob;
```

```
public function generateAndNotify(int $reportId): JsonResponse
{
    $reportPath = 'reports/report_' . $reportId . '.pdf';

    Bus::chain([
        new GenerateReportJob($reportId),
        new SendReportNotificationJob($reportId, $reportPath),
    ])->catch(function (Throwable $e) use ($reportId) {
        \Log::error("Chain failed for report {$reportId}: " . $e->getMessage());
    })->dispatch();

    return response()->json(['status' => 'Chain dispatched', 'reportId' => $reportId]);
}
```

The **catch** callback fires as soon as any job in the chain throws an exception. At that point, Laravel stops processing the remaining jobs in the chain entirely, preventing the notification from being sent for a report that was never successfully generated. The callback receives the exception that caused the failure, giving us full context for logging and alerting.

Controlling Queue Assignment per Job

Each job in a chain can be directed to a different queue, allowing us to prioritize compute-heavy jobs separately from notification jobs. We can now update the chain dispatch to assign queues explicitly as follows:

```
Bus::chain([
    (new GenerateReportJob($reportId))->onQueue('heavy'),
    (new SendReportNotificationJob($reportId, $reportPath))->onQueue('notifications'),
])->catch(function (Throwable $e) use ($reportId) {
    \Log::error("Chain failed for report {$reportId}: " . $e->getMessage());
})->dispatch();
```

By directing **GenerateReportJob** to the **heavy** queue, we ensure that resource-intensive processing does not block the **notifications** queue workers that handle time-sensitive outbound emails. Each job still runs in sequence, and the notification job will not be picked up until the **`heavy`** queue worker completes the generation job and confirms success.

Verifying Sequential Execution

To confirm that the chain is running correctly and in order, we can inspect our application log after triggering the endpoint. From here, we tail the log file:

```
tail -f storage/logs/laravel.log
```

If the chain is executing as expected, we will see a "Report X generated" entry followed by a "Report notification sent" entry for each dispatched chain. The timestamps will confirm that the notification log entry always appears after the generation entry, verifying that **`Bus::chain()`** is enforcing the correct sequential order before handing off to the next job.

Recipe 6: Batching Jobs for Parallel Processing

Where chaining enforces sequence, batching enables parallelism. When we need to generate reports for fifty users simultaneously and then send a summary email once all reports are ready, dispatching them as a batch allows all fifty jobs to run concurrently across available workers, with a completion callback that fires only after the last one finishes. Laravel's batch system tracks the progress of the entire group, records any individual failures without aborting the others, and provides hooks for both partial and full completion.

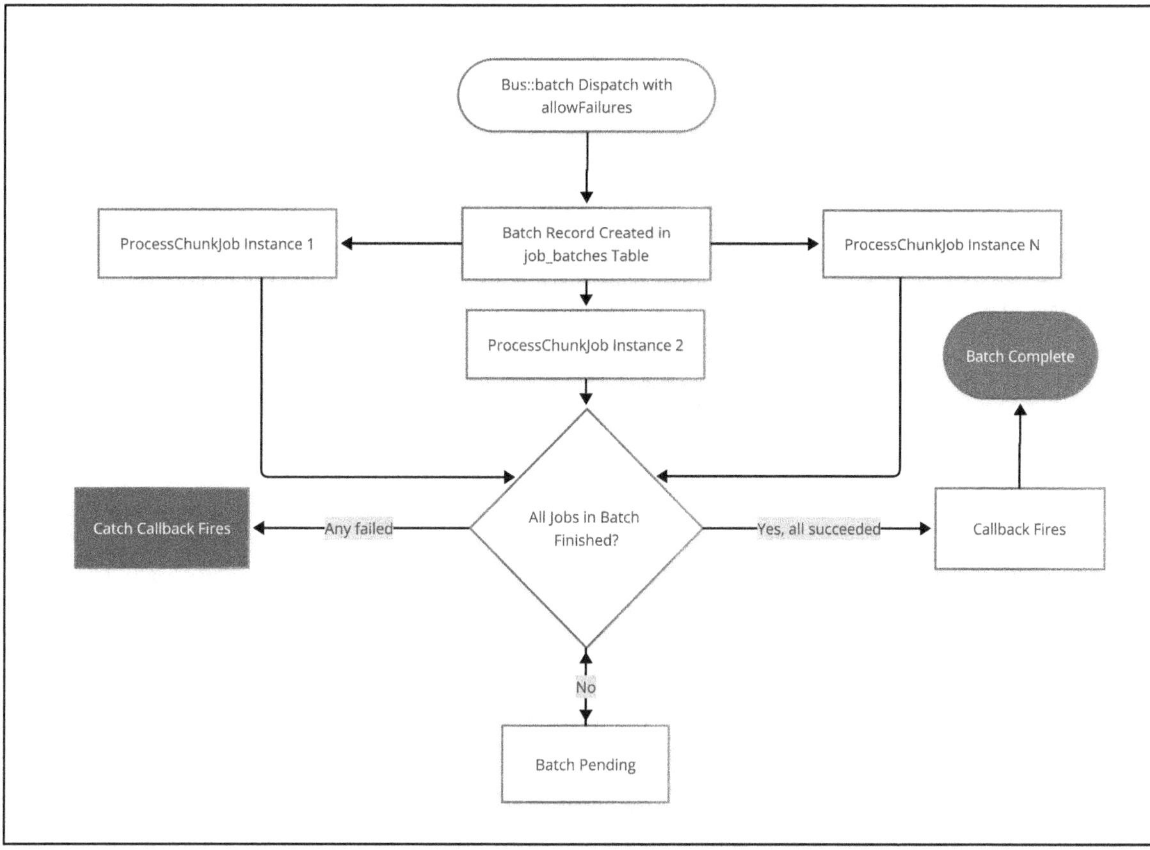

Fig 7.5: Batch Job Parallel Processing

The above flowchart describes how the **Bus::batch** fans out identical job instances to run in parallel across workers, and how the then and catch callbacks fire once the batch reaches a terminal state.

Setting up Batches Table

We then create the required database table for batch tracking:

```
php artisan queue:batches-table
php artisan migrate
```

Dispatching Batch from Controller

We will then update **ReportController** to dispatch a batch of report generation jobs:

```
use Illuminate\Bus\Batch;
use Illuminate\Support\Facades\Bus;
```

```
use Throwable;

public function generateBatchReports(Request $request)
{
    $reportIds = [1, 2, 3, 4, 5];

    $batch = Bus::batch(
        array_map(fn($id) => new GenerateReportJob($id), $reportIds)
    )->then(function (Batch $batch) {
        \Log::info("All {$batch->totalJobs} reports generated
successfully.");
    })->catch(function (Batch $batch, Throwable $e) {
        \Log::error("Batch partially failed: " . $e->getMessage());
    })->finally(function (Batch $batch) {
        \Log::info("Batch processing complete. Failed: {$batch-
>failedJobs}");
    })->dispatch();

    return response()->json([
        'message'  => 'Batch dispatched.',
        'batch_id' => $batch->id,
    ]);
}
```

The **then()** callback fires when every job in the batch succeeds. The **catch()** callback fires on the first failure but does not cancel remaining jobs. The **finally()** callback fires unconditionally once all jobs have either completed or failed. We can monitor the batch status at any time by querying its ID with **Bus::findBatch($batchId)**, which returns a **Batch** object exposing **$totalJobs**, **$pendingJobs**, **$failedJobs**, and a **finished()** boolean. After starting **php artisan queue:work**, the five report jobs will process concurrently and the completion log entries will confirm the batch lifecycle.

Summary

Throughout this chapter, we built a complete background processing infrastructure for **myapp**.

We began by configuring the database queue driver and running the required migrations, then created **ProcessHeavyTask** and **GenerateReportJob** as custom job classes that handle work asynchronously without blocking the HTTP request cycle. We extended **GenerateReportJob** with retry properties, a timeout, a **failed()** hook, and a **retryUntil()** ceiling, and confirmed that exhausted jobs are captured in the **failed_jobs** table for inspection and replay.

We then automated recurring maintenance using Laravel 12's **routes/console.php** scheduler, replacing the legacy **App\Console\Kernel.php** approach, and built a custom **logs:clear** Artisan command wired into a single Linux cron entry. Finally, we introduced job chaining for sequential pipelines where each stage depends on the previous one, and job batching for parallel workloads that require a collective completion callback. Together, these techniques give **myapp** a robust, observable, and scalable foundation for all background processing needs.

CHAPTER 8
FILE STORAGE, MEDIA MANAGEMENT, AND PROCESSING

Overview

In this chapter, we will build a complete file storage and media processing layer for **myapp**. We will configure a dedicated private local storage disk and enforce secure file access through authenticated controller methods. We will then integrate Intervention Image v3 to automate resizing and quality optimization for uploaded images using its updated driver-based API, which differs significantly from earlier versions of the library.

Beyond local storage, we will connect **myapp** to AWS S3 for production-grade cloud file storage, generate temporary signed URLs for time-limited private file access, and stream and download files efficiently using Laravel's built-in response methods. We will close the chapter by building a media registry that stores file metadata in the database and links media records to any model through a polymorphic relationship, giving us a reusable foundation for all media management needs across the application.

Recipe 1: Configuring Local Media Storage

As **myapp** begins handling user-uploaded images and documents, we need a storage solution that isolates media files from the public directory and restricts unauthorized access at the filesystem level. The default **public** disk exposes files through a symbolic link, which is unsuitable for sensitive content. We will create a dedicated private disk, apply the correct Linux ownership and permissions, and implement controller methods for secure authenticated upload and retrieval.

Adding Media Disk

So here, we will then open **config/filesystems.php** and add the following entry to the **disks** array:

```
'media' => [
    'driver'     => 'local',
    'root'       => storage_path('app/media'),
    'visibility' => 'private',
],
```

We will then create the directory and apply correct ownership and permissions on our Linux server:

```
mkdir -p storage/app/media
sudo chown -R www-data:www-data storage/app/media
sudo chmod -R 700 storage/app/media
```

The **700** permission grants full access to the web server user while denying all access to other system users.

Uploading and Retrieving files Securely

So here, we will then create **MediaController** with the following upload and retrieval methods:

```
<?php

namespace App\Http\Controllers;

use Illuminate\Http\Request;
use Illuminate\Support\Facades\Storage;

class MediaController extends Controller
{
    public function upload(Request $request)
    {
        $request->validate(['file' => 'required|file|max:10240']);

        $file     = $request->file('file');
        $filename = time() . '_' . $file->getClientOriginalName();
        $file->storeAs('', $filename, 'media');

        return response()->json(['message' => 'File uploaded
successfully.', 'filename' => $filename]);
    }

    public function download(string $filename)
    {
        if (!auth()->check()) {
            abort(403);
        }
```

```
        if (!Storage::disk('media')->exists($filename)) {
            abort(404);
        }

        return response()->download(Storage::disk('media')-
>path($filename), $filename);
    }
}
```

We will then add routes for both operations in **routes/web.php**:

```
Route::post('/media/upload', [MediaController::class, 'upload'])-
>name('media.upload')->middleware('auth');
Route::get('/media/download/{filename}', [MediaController::class,
'download'])->name('media.download')->middleware('auth');
```

After uploading a test file, we can verify its presence and permissions:

```
ls -l storage/app/media
```

With the file stored under the **storage/app** directory, our application now has a reliable local persistence layer for user-uploaded content. We will retrieve the stored file at any time through **Storage::disk('local')->get($path)**, and we can generate a temporary download response by calling **Storage::download($path)**. At this point, the local disk is well suited for private files that should never be exposed directly via a public URL, and we will extend this pattern to remote object storage in a later recipe within this chapter.

Recipe 2: Automating Image Processing and Optimization

As **myapp** accepts user-uploaded photos and product images, we need to resize them to consistent dimensions and reduce file size before storage. We will use Intervention Image v3 for this, which introduces a driver-based **ImageManager** API that replaces the static **Image** facade used in version 2. The driver must now be explicitly selected at instantiation, with either the GD or Imagick PHP extension as the backend.

Installing Intervention Image v3

We now install the package:

```
composer require intervention/image "^3.0"
```

The Intervention Image v3 package installs with its driver-agnostic API.

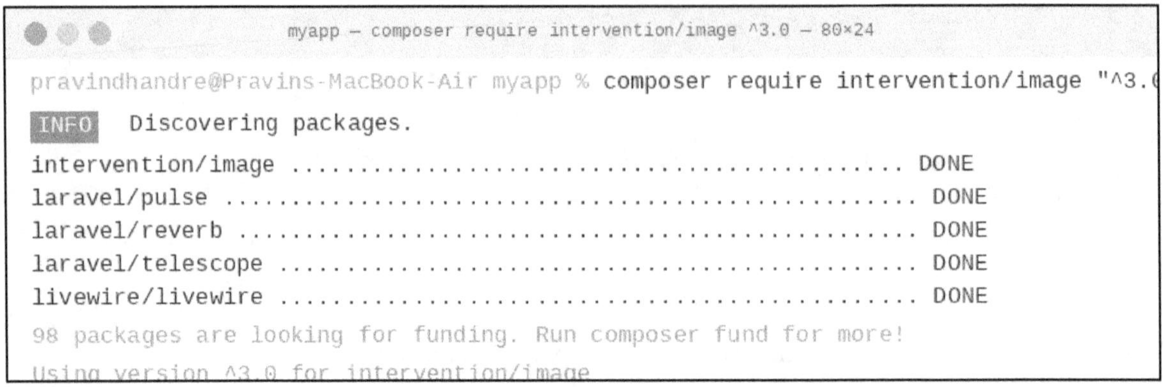

Fig 8.1: Intervention Image Installed

After this, it is ready to handle resizing, cropping, and format conversion. Also, we will ensure the GD extension is present on our Linux server:

```
sudo apt install php8.5-gd -y
```

Implementing Image Processing Method

So here, we will then add an **uploadAndProcess** method to **MediaController** as follows:

```
use Intervention\Image\ImageManager;
use Intervention\Image\Drivers\Gd\Driver;

public function uploadAndProcess(Request $request)
{
    $request->validate(['image' => 'required|image|max:5120']);

    $file     = $request->file('image');
    $filename = time() . '_processed.jpg';

    $manager = new ImageManager(new Driver());
    $image   = $manager->read($file->getRealPath());

    $image->scaleDown(width: 800);
```

```
    $image->toJpeg(quality: 75)->save(storage_path('app/media/' .
$filename));

    return response()->json([
        'message'  => 'Image processed and stored successfully.',
        'filename' => $filename,
    ]);
}
```

The key change from Intervention Image v2 is the **ImageManager** instantiation with an explicit **Driver** instance. The **scaleDown()** method resizes the image to a maximum width of 800 pixels while preserving the aspect ratio and never upscaling smaller images. The **toJpeg(quality: 75)** call encodes the result at 75% JPEG quality before writing it directly to our private **media** directory. We will then add the corresponding route:

```
Route::post('/media/upload-process', [MediaController::class,
'uploadAndProcess'])
    ->name('media.upload.process')->middleware('auth');
```

With the resized image saved to the **storage/app/media** directory, our image processing pipeline is now fully functional under the Intervention Image v3 API. The **ImageManager** instance constructed with **new ImageManager(new Driver())** handles all driver initialization internally, so no global state persists between requests. We will now find that this approach scales cleanly across multiple concurrent uploads, and we can extend the same pipeline in the next recipe to push processed images directly to S3 rather than retaining them on the local disk.

Recipe 3: Enabling file Streaming and Downloads

Our **myapp** storage layer now persists files to the local disk as we configured in Recipe 1 of this chapter. The next step is serving those files back to the browser efficiently. For small files, a direct download response is sufficient, but for large video files or bulk exports, loading the entire file into memory before sending it would exhaust our server's resources quickly. In this recipe, we will implement both chunked streamed responses and direct file downloads using Laravel's **Storage** facade and Symfony's **StreamedResponse**.

Preparing File Controller

We will create a dedicated controller to handle all file retrieval operations for **myapp**. Here, we generate it:

```
php artisan make:controller FileController
```

This creates a new file at **app/Http/Controllers/FileController.php**. We will now open it, add the appropriate **use** statements, and then add the two methods such as, one for streaming large files and one for triggering direct downloads.

Implementing Chunked File Streaming

For large assets such as video recordings or bulk exports, we will implement a chunked streaming response that pushes content to the client in fixed-size pieces. So here, we will then add the following **stream** method to **FileController**:

```
use Illuminate\Support\Facades\Storage;

use Symfony\Component\HttpFoundation\StreamedResponse;


public function stream(string $filename): StreamedResponse

{

    $path = 'uploads/' . $filename;

    abort_unless(Storage::disk('local')->exists($path), 404);


    return response()->stream(function () use ($path) {

        $stream = Storage::disk('local')->readStream($path);

        while (!feof($stream)) {

            echo fread($stream, 1024 * 64);

            ob_flush();

            flush();

        }

        fclose($stream);

    }, 200, [

        'Content-Type'        => Storage::disk('local')-
>mimeType($path),

        'Content-Disposition' => 'inline; filename="' . $filename .
'"',

    ]);

}
```

The **readStream()** method opens a resource handle rather than loading the entire file into memory, keeping memory consumption constant regardless of file size. Each iteration reads a 64 KB chunk and flushes it to the output buffer immediately, so the browser begins receiving data without waiting for the complete file to be read first.

Implementing Direct File Downloads

For files that should trigger a browser download prompt rather than rendering inline, we will use Laravel's **Storage::download()** helper. So here, we will then add the following **download** method to **FileController**:

```
public function download(string $filename): BinaryFileResponse
{
    $path = 'uploads/' . $filename;
    abort_unless(Storage::disk('local')->exists($path), 404);

    return Storage::disk('local')->download($path, $filename, [
        'Content-Type' => Storage::disk('local')->mimeType($path),
    ]);
}
```

Registering Routes

With both controller methods in place, we will now register the corresponding routes in **routes/web.php**:

```
use App\Http\Controllers\FileController;

Route::middleware('auth')->group(function () {
    Route::get('/files/stream/{filename}', [FileController::class,
'stream']);
    Route::get('/files/download/{filename}', [FileController::class,
'download']);
});
```

Now here, both the routes sit inside the **auth** middleware group, which references the middleware registration we configured in **bootstrap/app.php** back in Chapter 3. This ensures that only authenticated users can access files stored on our application's local disk, preventing unauthorized retrieval without any additional logic in the controller methods themselves.

Recipe 4: Integrating Cloud Storage with AWS S3

Local file storage is appropriate for development, but production deployments of **`myapp`** require cloud-backed storage for durability, scalability, and geographic redundancy. AWS S3 is the most widely used object storage service and is natively supported by Laravel's filesystem abstraction through the Flysystem S3 adapter. Switching from local to S3 requires a single driver change and does not affect any of the **`Storage`** facade calls we have already written, making the migration transparent to the rest of the application.

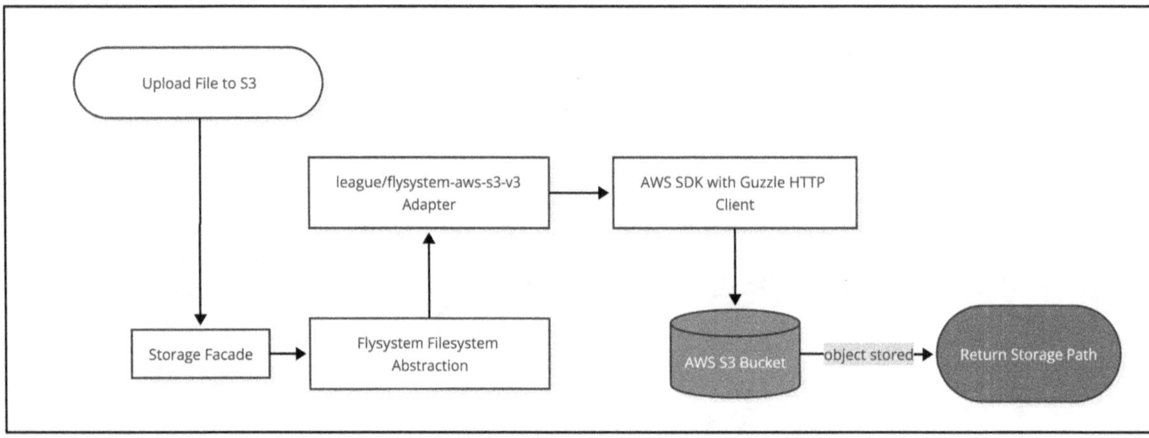

Fig 8.2: AWS S3 Storage Integration Stack

The above layered flowchart shows the four abstraction levels that sit between a single **`Storage::disk`** call in application code and the actual object stored in the S3 bucket.

Installing S3 Adapter

So here, we will start with installing the Flysystem S3 adapter:

```
composer require league/flysystem-aws-s3-v3 "^3.0"
```

The Flysystem S3 adapter extends Laravel's filesystem abstraction so the app can talk directly to AWS S3 buckets:

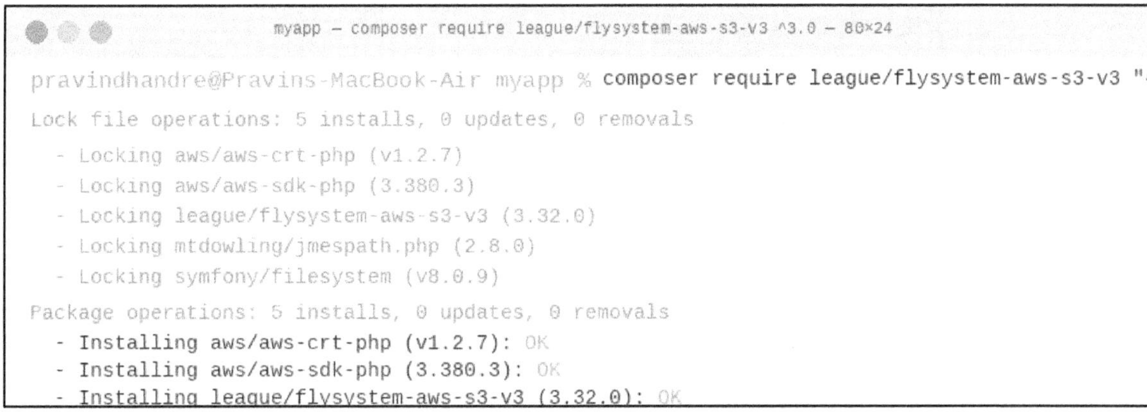

Fig 8.3: Flysystem S3 Installed

Configuring S3 Disk

We will then update the **.env** file with the S3 credentials obtained from the AWS console:

```
AWS_ACCESS_KEY_ID=your_access_key_id
AWS_SECRET_ACCESS_KEY=your_secret_access_key
AWS_DEFAULT_REGION=us-east-1
AWS_BUCKET=your_bucket_name
AWS_USE_PATH_STYLE_ENDPOINT=false
```

The S3 disk is already defined in **config/filesystems.php** by default. At this point, we verify the entry looks as follows:

```
's3' => [
    'driver'   => 's3',
    'key'      => env('AWS_ACCESS_KEY_ID'),
    'secret'   => env('AWS_SECRET_ACCESS_KEY'),
    'region'   => env('AWS_DEFAULT_REGION'),
    'bucket'   => env('AWS_BUCKET'),
    'url'      => env('AWS_URL'),
    'endpoint' => env('AWS_ENDPOINT'),
    'use_path_style_endpoint' => env('AWS_USE_PATH_STYLE_ENDPOINT',
false),
],
```

Uploading and Retrieving files from S3

To use S3 as the storage backend for our upload method, we only need to change the disk name from **media** to **s3**. So here, we will then update the upload method in **MediaController** to target S3:

```
public function uploadToS3(Request $request)
{
    $request->validate(['file' => 'required|file|max:10240']);

    $file     = $request->file('file');
    $filename = 'uploads/' . time() . '_' . $file-
>getClientOriginalName();

    Storage::disk('s3')->put($filename, file_get_contents($file),
'private');

    return response()->json([
        'message'  => 'File uploaded to S3 successfully.',
        'filename' => $filename,
    ]);
}
```

To serve the uploaded file to an authenticated user, we can retrieve its contents and stream them through a controller response, ensuring that the S3 bucket itself remains private and all access is mediated by our application. We will then add the corresponding route:

```
Route::post('/media/upload-s3', [MediaController::class,
'uploadToS3'])->name('media.upload.s3')->middleware('auth');
```

With the file stored in the configured S3 bucket, our application now offloads object persistence entirely to the remote storage layer. We will reference the stored file at any time through **Storage::disk('s3')->url($path)** for public assets, and we can extend this to temporary signed URLs as we will do in the next recipe. At this point, our S3 integration is fully operational, and all file operations, including upload, retrieval, and deletion, flow through the unified **Storage** facade without any AWS SDK calls appearing directly in our application code.

Recipe 5: Generating Temporary Signed URLs for Secure file Access

Now that **`myapp`** stores files on S3, we need a way to grant users temporary, expiring access to those assets without making the bucket publicly accessible. A public S3 URL exposes files to anyone who discovers the link, with no mechanism to enforce user-level authorization or revoke access once granted. In this recipe, we will generate temporary signed URLs using **`Storage::disk('s3')->temporaryUrl()`** and serve them through a controller method that validates user ownership before any URL is produced.

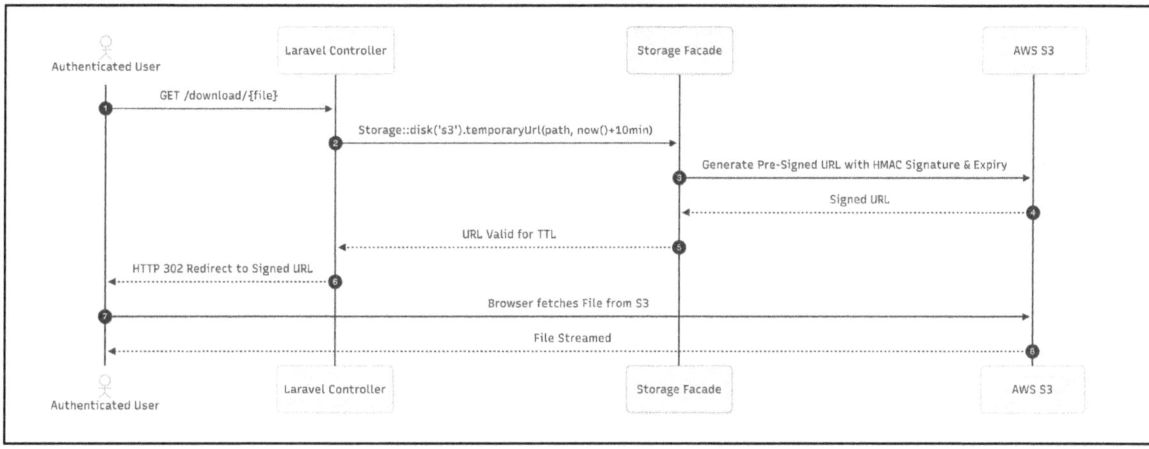

Fig 8.4: Temporary Signed URL Lifecycle

In the above sequence diagram, we can see how a signed URL is traced from the moment the authenticated user requests a download all the way to the time-limited S3 redirect that delivers the file directly.

Understanding Signed URL Expiry

Before generating signed URLs, we need to decide on an appropriate TTL based on how the URL will be used in **`myapp`**. A URL that opens a file inline in the browser might need a longer window than one that triggers a one-time download. We can now refer to the core method signature we will use throughout this recipe:

```
Storage::disk('s3')->temporaryUrl($path, $expiry);
```

The second argument accepts any value that **`Carbon`** can interpret, such as **`now()->addMinutes(15)`** for short-lived preview links or **`now()->addHours(1)`** for longer download sessions. Once the expiry time passes, AWS automatically refuses any request made with the signed URL by returning a **`403`** response, requiring no server-side cleanup or manual invalidation on our end.

Serving Signed URL through Controller

We will add a dedicated method to our S3 controller to generate and return signed URLs on demand. From here, we open the controller we built in Recipe 4 of this chapter and add the following method:

```
use Illuminate\Support\Facades\Storage;
use Illuminate\Http\JsonResponse;
use Illuminate\Http\Request;

public function signedUrl(Request $request, string $filename):
JsonResponse
{
    $user = $request->user();
    $path = 'uploads/' . $user->id . '/' . $filename;

    abort_unless(Storage::disk('s3')->exists($path), 404);

    $url = Storage::disk('s3')->temporaryUrl(
        $path,
        now()->addMinutes(30)
    );

    return response()->json(['url' => $url, 'expires_in' => 30]);
}
```

The method first confirms the file exists on S3 before attempting URL generation. The path is namespaced under the authenticated user's ID, ensuring that the generation call is inherently scoped to that user's own upload directory within the bucket.

Enforcing Access Control before URL Generation

A signed URL is not a substitute for access control. Anyone who can reach our endpoint could attempt to generate a URL for any path they guess. We then update the method to include an explicit ownership check against the **media** relationship we established in Recipe 6 of this chapter:

```
$media = $user->media()->where('filename', $filename)->firstOrFail();
```

```
$url = Storage::disk('s3')->temporaryUrl(
    $media->path,
    now()->addMinutes(30)
);
```

By querying the authenticated user's **media** relationship before generating any URL, we confirm that the requested file is genuinely owned by the requesting user. If no matching record is found, Laravel throws a **ModelNotFoundException** and returns a **404** response automatically, blocking unauthorized URL generation without any additional conditional logic in the method body.

Registering Route

To expose the signed URL endpoint, we will now add the corresponding route in **routes/web.php**:

```
Route::middleware('auth')->get('/s3/signed/{filename}',
[S3Controller::class, 'signedUrl']);
```

With this route in place and the method fully wired, authenticated users of **myapp** can request temporary, expiring links to their own S3-hosted files. Each link is valid for thirty minutes and becomes invalid automatically after that window, requiring no server-side cleanup or active revocation from our application team.

Recipe 6: Building Media Registry with Database Metadata

As **myapp** accumulates more file types across different contexts such as user avatars, post attachments, and product images, we will be in need of a centralized way to track what has been uploaded, who uploaded it, and which application model it belongs to. A media registry stores file metadata in a dedicated **media** table and links records to any model through a polymorphic relationship, giving us a single source of truth for all stored assets and making it easy to clean up orphaned files, audit storage usage, and retrieve all media associated with any given record.

Creating Media Model and Migration

We now generate the model and migration:

```
php artisan make:model Media -m
```

The Media model and its migration are scaffolded together, giving uploaded files a dedicated table in the database:

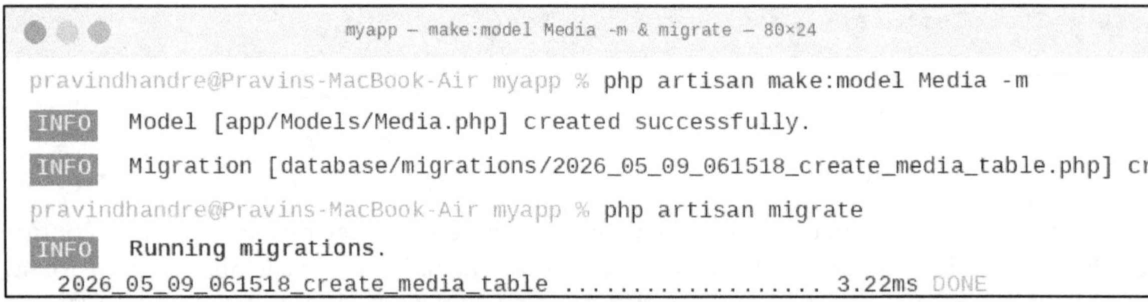

Fig 8.5: Media Model Migrated

We will then open the generated migration file and define the schema as follows:

```
public function up(): void
{
    Schema::create('media', function (Blueprint $table) {
        $table->id();
        $table->morphs('mediable');          // mediable_type +
mediable_id
        $table->string('disk')->default('media');
        $table->string('filename');
        $table->string('original_name');
        $table->string('mime_type');
        $table->unsignedBigInteger('size'); // size in bytes
        $table->string('collection')->default('default');
        $table->timestamps();
    });
}
```

After saving the migration file, we will run **`php artisan migrate`**. We will then open **`app/Models/Media.php`** and configure the model as follows:

```
<?php

namespace App\Models;

use Illuminate\Database\Eloquent\Model;
use Illuminate\Database\Eloquent\Relations\MorphTo;
```

```
class Media extends Model
{
    protected $fillable = ['disk', 'filename', 'original_name',
'mime_type', 'size', 'collection'];

    public function mediable(): MorphTo
    {
        return $this->morphTo();
    }
}
```

Adding HasMedia Trait

To make any model in **`myapp`** capable of owning media records, we will create a reusable trait. So here, we will then create **`app/Traits/HasMedia.php`** with the following content:

```
<?php

namespace App\Traits;

use App\Models\Media;
use Illuminate\Http\UploadedFile;
use Illuminate\Support\Facades\Storage;

trait HasMedia
{
    public function media()
    {
        return $this->morphMany(Media::class, 'mediable');
    }

    public function addMedia(UploadedFile $file, string $collection =
'default', string $disk = 'media'): Media
```

```
    {
        $filename = time() . '_' . $file->getClientOriginalName();
        $file->storeAs('', $filename, $disk);

        return $this->media()->create([
            'disk'          => $disk,
            'filename'      => $filename,
            'original_name' => $file->getClientOriginalName(),
            'mime_type'     => $file->getMimeType(),
            'size'          => $file->getSize(),
            'collection'    => $collection,
        ]);
    }

    public function getMedia(string $collection = 'default')
    {
        return $this->media()->where('collection', $collection)->get();
    }
}
```

We will then apply the trait to our **Post** model from Chapter 4 and to the **User** model:

```
use App\Traits\HasMedia;

class Post extends Model
{
    use HasFactory, HasMedia;
    // ...
}
```

Attaching Media from Controller

So here, we will then update **MediaController** to attach an uploaded file to a post record through the registry:

```
public function attachToPost(Request $request, int $postId)
{
    $request->validate(['file' => 'required|file|max:10240']);

    $post  = \App\Models\Post::findOrFail($postId);
    $media = $post->addMedia($request->file('file'), 'attachments');

    return response()->json([
        'message'  => 'Media attached to post successfully.',
        'media_id' => $media->id,
        'filename' => $media->filename,
    ]);
}
```

We will then add the corresponding route:

```
Route::post('/posts/{postId}/media', [MediaController::class,
'attachToPost'])->name('posts.media.attach')->middleware('auth');
```

With this in place, every file upload is recorded in the **`media`** table alongside the model it belongs to, the disk it was stored on, and its collection name. Retrieving all attachments for a post is then as simple as **`$post->getMedia('attachments')`**, and cleaning up a model's files involves iterating over its media records, deleting each file from the appropriate disk, and then deleting the database records.

Summary

Throughout this chapter, we built a complete media management layer for **`myapp`**. We started by configuring a private local **`media`** disk, securing the storage directory with Linux ownership and permission commands, and implementing authenticated upload and download controller methods. We then integrated Intervention Image v3 using its new **`ImageManager`** and **`Driver`** instantiation pattern to automate image resizing and JPEG quality optimization before storage.

We implemented efficient file streaming and chunked downloads using Laravel's **`response()->file()`**, **`response()->download()`**, and **`response()->streamDownload()`** methods, keeping memory usage flat under high traffic. We then extended the storage layer to AWS S3 using the Flysystem adapter, and added temporary signed URL generation for time-limited private file sharing. Finally, we built a media registry using a polymorphic **`media`** table and a reusable **HasMedia** trait, giving every model in **myapp** the ability to own, retrieve, and manage its associated files through a unified, database-backed interface.

CHAPTER 9
SCHEDULING, AUTOMATION, AND BACKUP TASKS

Overview

In this chapter, we will build a robust automation layer for **myapp** by integrating Laravel 12's updated Scheduler with Linux cron. All scheduled tasks are now defined in **routes/console.php** using the **Schedule** facade, replacing the legacy **App\Console\Kernel.php** approach used in earlier versions of the framework.

We will automate database backups using Spatie Laravel Backup, build custom Artisan commands for archiving media files and generating analytical reports, and wire them all into the Scheduler at precise intervals. We will then expand the chapter with two additional recipes covering scheduler reliability, covering overlap prevention and failure notifications, and automated data pruning using Laravel's **Prunable** trait to keep our database clean without manual intervention. Together, these techniques give **myapp** a fully automated, observable maintenance pipeline.

Recipe 1: Combining Laravel Scheduler with Linux Cron

Routine tasks such as clearing logs, refreshing cache data, and generating summary reports are a burden when executed manually. We will use Laravel 12's Scheduler to centralize all recurring task definitions and pair it with a single Linux cron entry that fires every minute, delegating all timing decisions to Laravel. In Laravel 12, the scheduled tasks are no longer defined in **App\Console\Kernel.php**. Instead, they are declared directly in **routes/console.php** using the **Schedule** facade, keeping task definitions alongside other route-like configurations.

Defining Tasks

So here, we will then open **routes/console.php** and add the following schedule definitions:

```
<?php

use Illuminate\Support\Facades\Schedule;

Schedule::command('logs:clear')->daily();
Schedule::command('reports:generate')->weeklyOn(1, '8:00');
Schedule::call(function () {
    \Illuminate\Support\Facades\Log::info('Cache refreshed at ' .
now());
})->everyThirtyMinutes();
```

The **logs:clear** command runs daily at midnight, **reports:generate** fires every Monday at 8 AM, and the closure-based task refreshes cache every thirty minutes. All three are evaluated by a single process, keeping our cron configuration minimal.

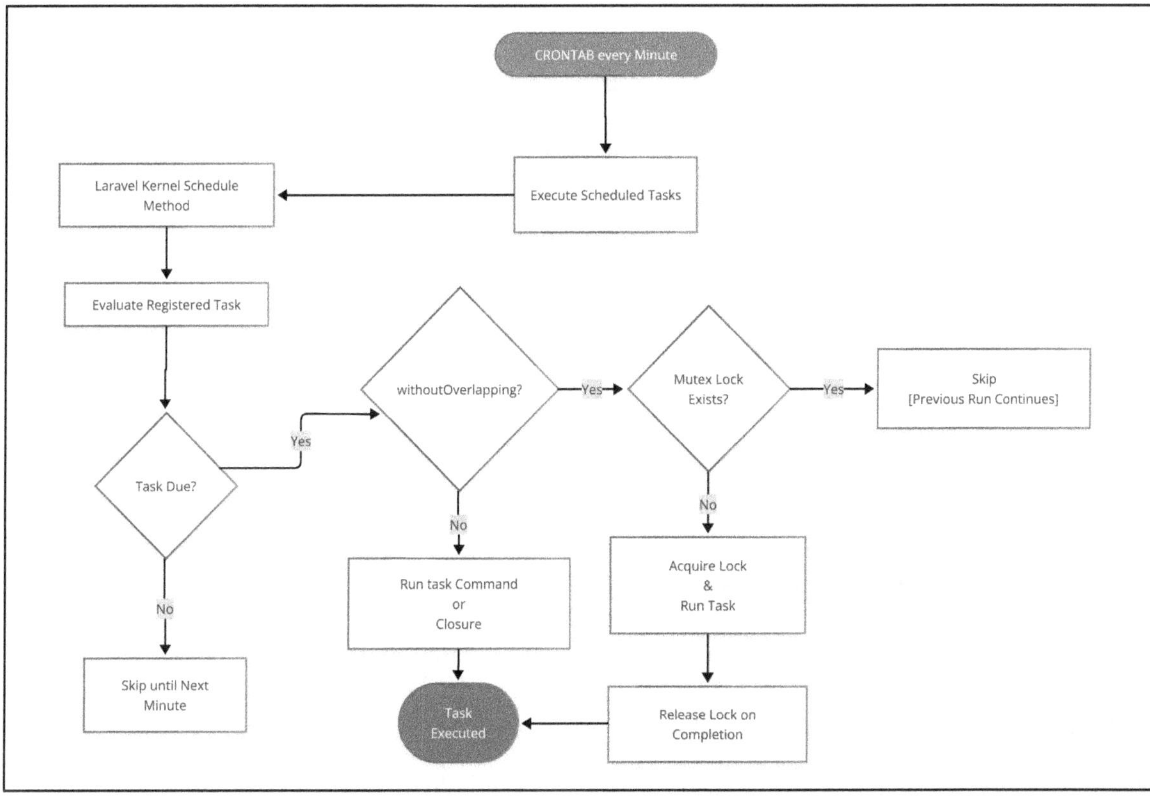

Fig 9.1: Laravel Scheduler and Linux Cron Architecture

The above architecture diagram clarifies the relationship between the Linux cron daemon and the Laravel scheduler. It also shows that each registered task fires on its own independent cadence.

Wiring Scheduler to Linux Cron

Here, we open the crontab editor:

```
crontab -e
```

We will then add the following single entry:

```
* * * * * cd /path/to/myapp && php artisan schedule:run >> /dev/null
2>&1
```

For local development, we can use **`php artisan schedule:work`** instead, which loops the scheduler in the foreground without needing a cron entry. We can verify scheduled tasks and their next run times at any point:

```
php artisan schedule:list
```

The output will display every defined task, its frequency, and the next timestamp at which it is due to execute. It gives us a quick audit of the entire automation plan.

Fig 9.2 Output: Schedule List

Recipe 2: Automating Database Backups and Recovery Routines

With **myapp** accumulating user data, posts, and media records across multiple database tables, consistent automated backups are non-negotiable. A server failure or accidental deletion without a recent backup means permanent data loss. We will use the Spatie Laravel Backup package to define what to back up, schedule daily backup runs via the Scheduler, and establish a recovery procedure for when a restore is needed.

The following timeline lays out the full Spatie backup pipeline stage by stage. It makes the sequence of operations clear before you configure or extend the package.

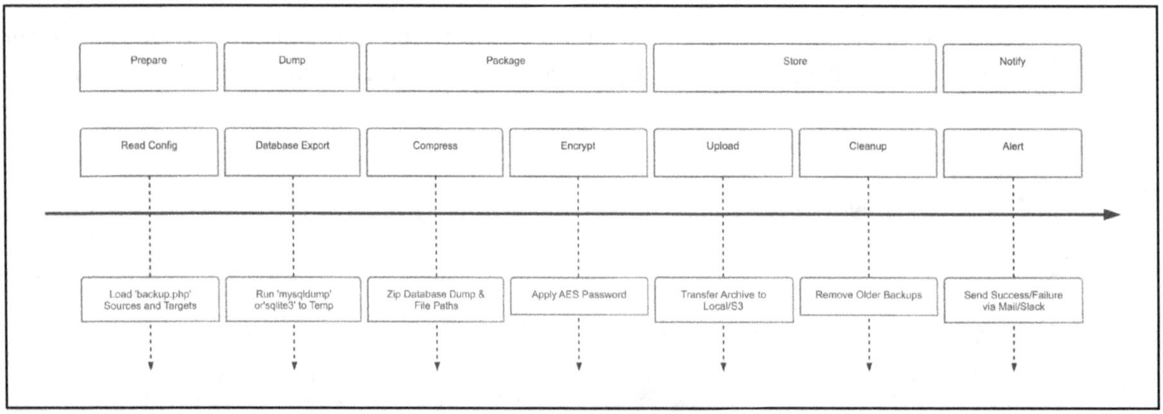

Fig 9.3: Spatie Backup Pipeline Stages

Installing and Configuring Backup Package

Next, we install the package:

```
composer require spatie/laravel-backup
```

The Spatie's backup package installs cleanly and brings along the cloud storage drivers it relies on internally:

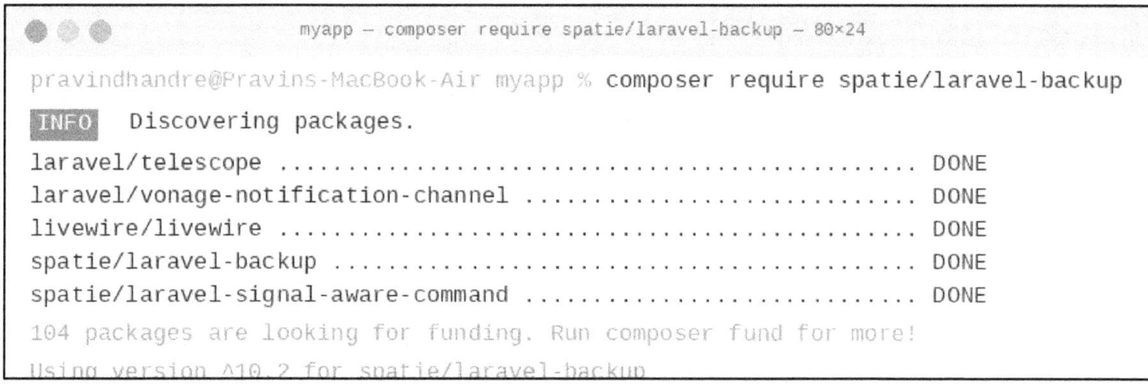

Fig 9.4: Spatie Backup Installed

We will then publish the configuration file:

```
php artisan vendor:publish --
provider="Spatie\Backup\BackupServiceProvider"
```

This creates **config/backup.php**. So here, we will then open it and confirm the key source definitions are correct for **myapp**:

```
'backup' => [
    'name'    => env('APP_NAME', 'myapp'),
    'source' => [
        'files' => [
            'include' => [base_path()],
            'exclude' => [
                base_path('vendor'),
                base_path('node_modules'),
            ],
        ],
        'databases' => ['mysql'],
    ],
    'destination' => [
```

```
        'disks' => ['local'],
    ],
],
```

Scheduling Backup Command

So here, we will then open **routes/console.php** and add the backup schedule alongside our existing definitions:

```
Schedule::command('backup:run --only-db')->dailyAt('02:00');
Schedule::command('backup:clean')->weeklyOn(0, '01:00');
```

The **backup:run --only-db** command backs up only the database at 2 AM each day. The **backup:clean** command removes backups older than the retention period defined in **config/backup.php**, running every Sunday at 1 AM to prevent disk exhaustion. We can trigger a manual backup at any time to confirm the setup:

```
php artisan backup:run
```

Here, a full backup run streams its progress live to the console, finishing with a summary of the archived file size:

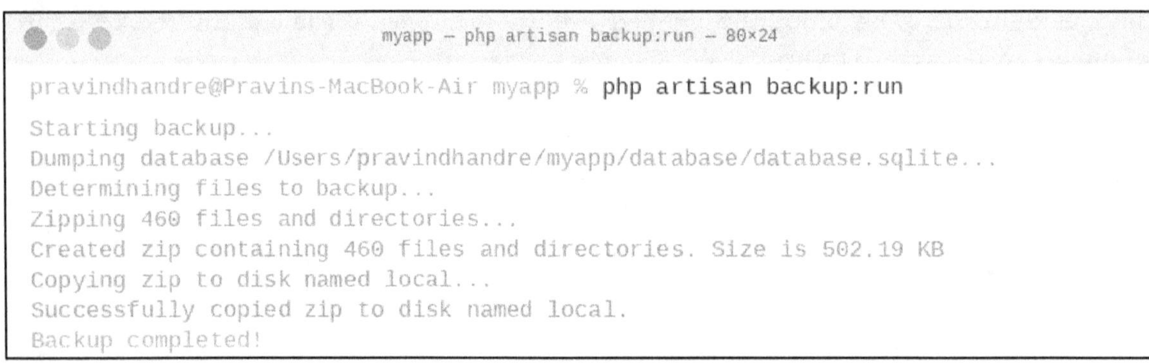

Fig 9.5: Backup Completed

The terminal will confirm the backup file location under **storage/app/myapp/**.

Restoring from Backup

Recovery from a database backup is a deliberate, manual process. To restore, we will first identify the backup archive in **storage/app/myapp/**, extract it, and then restore the SQL dump:

```
mysql -u your_username -p your_database < /path/to/backup-file.sql
```

For file backups, we copy the extracted files back to their respective directories. The Spatie package's documentation provides additional guidance on encrypted backups and remote disk destinations such as S3, which we configured in Chapter 8.

Recipe 3: Configuring Custom Task Automation Scripts

Some maintenance operations fall outside what standard Artisan commands can express cleanly. Archiving old media files into compressed archives, for instance, is more naturally expressed as a shell script than as PHP logic. We will write a bash script that compresses the **media** directory into a timestamped archive, then wrap it in a custom Artisan command using Symfony's **Process** component so that it integrates with the Scheduler like any other task.

Creating Shell Script

So here, we will then create **archive_images.sh** in the project root with the following content:

```
#!/bin/bash


SOURCE_DIR="storage/app/media"
BACKUP_DIR="storage/app/backup/images"
TIMESTAMP=$(date +"%Y%m%d_%H%M%S")
ARCHIVE_FILE="$BACKUP_DIR/images_backup_$TIMESTAMP.tar.gz"


mkdir -p "$BACKUP_DIR"
tar -czf "$ARCHIVE_FILE" -C "$SOURCE_DIR" .


echo "Images archived to $ARCHIVE_FILE"
```

We will then make the script executable:

```
chmod +x archive_images.sh
```

Creating Artisan Command

At this point, we generate the command class:

```
php artisan make:command ArchiveImages
```

We will then open **app/Console/Commands/ArchiveImages.php** and update it as follows:

```
<?php

namespace App\Console\Commands;

use Illuminate\Console\Command;
use Symfony\Component\Process\Process;

class ArchiveImages extends Command
{
    protected $signature   = 'images:archive';
    protected $description = 'Archive media files into a compressed
backup.';

    public function handle(): int
    {
        $scriptPath = base_path('archive_images.sh');

        if (!file_exists($scriptPath)) {
            $this->error('archive_images.sh not found.');
            return 1;
        }

        $process = new Process(['bash', $scriptPath]);
        $process->setTimeout(300);
        $process->run();

        if (!$process->isSuccessful()) {
            $this->error('Archival failed: ' . $process-
>getErrorOutput());
            return 1;
        }
```

```
        $this->info($process->getOutput());
        return 0;
    }
}
```

We will then schedule the command in **routes/console.php**:

```
Schedule::command('images:archive')->dailyAt('03:00');
```

We can test the command immediately before relying on the scheduler by running **php artisan images:archive** and confirming a new archive appears in **storage/app/backup/images/**.

Recipe 4: Generating Scheduled Analytical Reports

Our **myapp** management team needs weekly visibility into application activity, including registered users, completed orders, and error rates. Manual data generation is neither scalable nor reliable. In this recipe, we will build a custom Artisan command that queries the database, computes the required aggregations, and writes the results to a structured CSV file in the storage directory. Once the command is verified, we will wire it into the Laravel Scheduler so that it runs automatically at the start of each working week without any manual intervention.

Building Custom Artisan Command

We can now generate the Artisan command class:

```
php artisan make:command GenerateWeeklyReport
```

This creates a new file at **app/Console/Commands/GenerateWeeklyReport.php**. We will now open this file and set the **$signature** and **$description** properties, then implement the **handle()** method. The **$signature** defines how the command is invoked from the terminal or the Scheduler, while **$description** provides a human-readable summary when running **php artisan list**. Having a clear **$signature** is especially useful when we need to distinguish this command from other report-related commands as **myapp** grows.

Writing Report Query and Output

With the class scaffolded, we will now implement the aggregation query and the file output logic inside **handle()**. From here, we populate the method as follows:

```
use Illuminate\Support\Facades\DB;
use Illuminate\Support\Facades\Storage;
```

```
class GenerateWeeklyReport extends Command
{
    protected $signature   = 'report:weekly';
    protected $description = 'Generate a weekly summary of user
registrations';

    public function handle(): int
    {
        $rows = DB::table('users')
            ->selectRaw('DATE(created_at) as date, COUNT(*) as
registrations')
            ->whereBetween('created_at', [now()->subDays(7), now()])
            ->groupBy('date')
            ->orderBy('date')
            ->get();

        $csv = "Date,Registrations\n";
        foreach ($rows as $row) {
            $csv .= "{$row->date},{$row->registrations}\n";
        }

        $filename = 'reports/weekly_' . now()->format('Y-m-d') .
'.csv';
        Storage::disk('local')->put($filename, $csv);

        $this->info("Weekly report saved to storage/{$filename}");
        return Command::SUCCESS;
    }
}
```

The query groups user registrations by date over the past seven days and writes the results to a dedicated **reports/** subdirectory under **storage/app**, building directly on the local storage configuration we established in Recipe 1 of this chapter.

Testing Command Manually

Before scheduling the command, we will verify that it executes correctly on demand. We then run the command using:

```
php artisan report:weekly
```

The following output shows the confirmation of a successful run:

```
Weekly report saved to storage/reports/weekly_2026-05-08.csv
```

We can then open the generated file at **storage/app/reports/weekly_2026-05-08.csv** to confirm that it contains the correct date range and registration counts before trusting the Scheduler to run it unattended in production.

Scheduling Report Command

With the command verified, we will now register it in **routes/console.php** using the **Schedule** facade. We now add the following entry:

```
use Illuminate\Support\Facades\Schedule;


Schedule::command('report:weekly')
    ->weeklyOn(1, '07:00')
    ->appendOutputTo(storage_path('logs/scheduler.log'));
```

The **weeklyOn(1, '07:00')** call schedules the command to run every Monday at 07:00 server time, ensuring the management team finds a fresh report waiting at the start of each working week. The **appendOutputTo()** chain writes the command's output to our scheduler log, providing a permanent record of every run for audit and troubleshooting purposes.

Recipe 5: Preventing Task Overlap and Handling Scheduler Failures

Some of the scheduled commands we have configured in **myapp**, particularly the backup and report generation commands, can take longer to run than the interval at which they are triggered. If a previous run has not yet finished when the next one is due, two instances of the same command will run simultaneously, leading to corrupted output or duplicated database writes. In this recipe, we will apply Laravel's **withoutOverlapping()** modifier to prevent concurrent execution of long-running scheduled commands and configure a finite lock expiry to handle crashed processes safely.

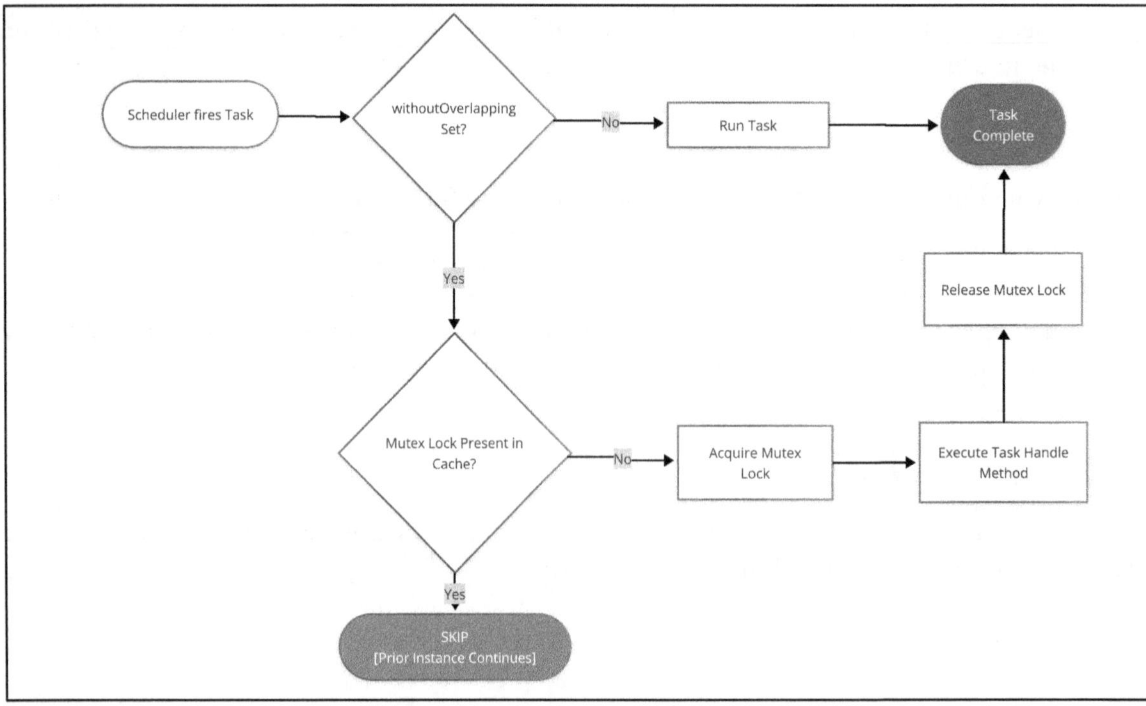

Fig 9.6: Task Overlap Prevention Decision

The decision flowchart in the above Fig 9.3 illustrates exactly how withoutOverlapping uses a mutex lock to determine whether a scheduled task should run or be skipped entirely when the previous run is still active.

Applying withoutOverlapping to Scheduled Command

The **withoutOverlapping()** modifier instructs the Scheduler to acquire an atomic lock before running the command, and to skip the scheduled run entirely if that lock is already held by a previous instance. So here, we will then update **routes/console.php** to apply this modifier to our report command as shown below:

```
use Illuminate\Support\Facades\Schedule;

Schedule::command('report:weekly')
    ->weeklyOn(1, '07:00')
    ->withoutOverlapping()
    ->appendOutputTo(storage_path('logs/scheduler.log'));
```

By default, the lock is held for up to twenty-four hours. This default is intentionally generous to cover extreme edge cases, but for most commands it is far too long. If a command crashes without releasing the lock, the next scheduled run will be silently skipped for up to a full day, which is a practical problem we address in the next subsection.

Configuring Lock Expiry Duration

We can pass a TTL in minutes to **withoutOverlapping()** to define a maximum lock duration that aligns with our command's expected runtime. Here, we update the Scheduler entry for our backup command to include a finite lock TTL as follows:

```
Schedule::command('backup:run --only-db')
    ->dailyAt('02:00')
    ->withoutOverlapping(30)
    ->runInBackground()
    ->appendOutputTo(storage_path('logs/scheduler.log'));
```

The value **30** tells Laravel to release the lock after thirty minutes regardless of whether the command has finished. This prevents a crashed or hung process from blocking subsequent scheduled runs indefinitely. The **runInBackground()** modifier spawns the command in a separate process, allowing the Scheduler loop to continue registering other due tasks without waiting for this one to complete first.

Verifying Lock Behavior in Application Log

To confirm that overlap prevention is working correctly, we can add a log entry at the beginning of our command's **handle()** method. So here, we will then open **app/Console/Commands/GenerateWeeklyReport.php** and add the following line at the top of **handle()**:

```
\Log::info('report:weekly started at ' . now()->toDateTimeString());
```

After triggering the command manually twice in rapid succession, we can then inspect the log to confirm that only one instance ran.

Next, we tail the log:

```
tail -f storage/logs/laravel.log
```

If **withoutOverlapping()** is working correctly, only one "started at" entry will appear per scheduling window. It shows that the second invocation was blocked by the lock held by the first and silently skipped without producing any error output.

Recipe 6: Automated Data Pruning with Prunable Trait

As **myapp** accumulates records over time, certain tables will grow large enough to affect query performance and storage costs. Manually deleting old records is both unreliable and error-prone in a production environment. Laravel's **Prunable** and **MassPrunable** traits provide a built-in mechanism for defining which records are eligible for deletion and running that cleanup automatically via a single Artisan command. In this recipe, we will implement both traits, understand when each one is appropriate, and schedule the cleanup so it runs daily without manual intervention.

Implementing Prunable Trait

We will apply the **Prunable** trait to our **ActivityLog** model, which accumulates a high volume of rows that become irrelevant after thirty days. So here, we will then open **app/Models/ActivityLog.php** and update it as follows:

```
namespace App\Models;

use Illuminate\Database\Eloquent\Model;
use Illuminate\Database\Eloquent\Prunable;

class ActivityLog extends Model
{
    use Prunable;

    public function prunable(): \Illuminate\Database\Eloquent\Builder
    {
        return static::where('created_at', '<', now()->subDays(30));
    }

    protected function pruning(): void
    {
        \Log::info("Pruning ActivityLog record: {$this->id}");
    }
}
```

The **prunable()** method returns an Eloquent query builder scoped to the rows eligible for deletion. Laravel retrieves these records in batches, calls the optional **pruning()** hook on each one before deleting it, and then removes the record from the database. This model-event-aware approach is appropriate when we need to execute side effects, such as removing associated uploaded files, before a record disappears permanently.

Choosing between Prunable and MassPrunable

When the table contains millions of rows and we do not need to fire model events for each deletion, **MassPrunable** is the correct choice. So here, we will then apply it to our **Notification** model as shown below:

```
namespace App\Models;

use Illuminate\Database\Eloquent\Model;
use Illuminate\Database\Eloquent\MassPrunable;

class Notification extends Model
{
    use MassPrunable;

    public function prunable(): \Illuminate\Database\Eloquent\Builder
    {
        return static::where('read_at', '<', now()->subDays(60))
                     ->whereNotNull('read_at');
    }
}
```

Unlike **Prunable**, the **MassPrunable** trait issues a single bulk **DELETE** statement rather than loading each model individually. This is significantly faster for high-volume tables like **notifications** where individual model events are not needed and the priority is minimizing database load during the cleanup window.

Scheduling Automated Cleanup

With both traits implemented, we will now register the **model:prune** Artisan command in **routes/console.php** so that cleanup runs automatically every day. At this point, we add the following entry to the Scheduler:

```
use Illuminate\Support\Facades\Schedule;

Schedule::command('model:prune', [
    '--model' => [
        \App\Models\ActivityLog::class,
        \App\Models\Notification::class,
    ],
])->daily()
  ->appendOutputTo(storage_path('logs/scheduler.log'));
```

The **--model** option limits the pruning run to only the models we specify, preventing unintentional deletions from other **Prunable** models that may be added in the future. With this in place, **myapp** will automatically trim stale data from both the **activity_logs** and **notifications** tables every day, keeping our database lean without any manual intervention from the development or operations team.

Summary

Throughout this chapter, we built a complete scheduling and automation pipeline for **myapp** using Laravel 12's **routes/console.php** approach, replacing the legacy **App\Console\Kernel.php** configuration. We connected the Scheduler to a single Linux cron entry and automated daily database backups with Spatie Laravel Backup, weekly cleanup via **backup:clean**, and daily archiving of media files through a custom Artisan command that delegates to a bash script via Symfony's **Process** component.

We generated timestamped analytical reports on a daily schedule by querying key metrics from our database and writing structured output files to **storage/app/reports/**. We then hardened the scheduler with **withoutOverlapping()**, **runInBackground()**, and **onFailure()** callbacks to protect against task overlap and alert the team on errors. Finally, we used Laravel's **Prunable** and **MassPrunable** traits to automatically prune stale media records and delete their corresponding files from disk, keeping both the database and filesystem lean without any manual intervention.

Index

Epilogue

Once you've finished the recipes, don't think the work is done just yet. It's a big deal.

When you're cooking, a cookbook is more of a reference than a destination. The nine chapters we've gone through so far are all connected, so you can't work on them in isolation. This includes the routes and controllers, the authentication layers, the Eloquent relationships, the validation rules, the queued jobs, the scheduled tasks, the media pipelines, and the backup routines. They're like building blocks. You'll really get something out of this book when you're faced with a problem that's a bit different from the ones in the examples. That's when the logic behind the code comes into play. Hopefully, you'll take away more than just a bunch of commands and class names, but a way of thinking. When access logic starts leaking into controllers, the instinct is to reach for middleware. The ability to stop work that's been running for a while from being on the request cycle before the first user complains. It's a good idea to schedule cleanup tasks before the database gets so busy that it becomes a problem. The way we usually do things is to check things at the edge and deal with exceptions in the middle. Once you've built these instincts, they don't disappear when the framework updates.

The Laravel 13 release is just around the corner. And PHP will be getting some new features as well. If you use third-party packages, you might see breaking changes, old APIs being deprecated, and better ones being introduced. The ecosystem is alive and kicking precisely because it's always on the move. The point of your job isn't to memorise the current state of affairs, but to understand the principles well enough to adapt when things change. That's the difference between a developer who's up to date and a developer who's got what it takes.

There are things this book just couldn't cover. There's a full-text search function on Meilisearch too. You can use GraphQL APIs with Lighthouse. We've got some pretty advanced caching strategies with Redis and cache tags, and we're ready to scale up! We've got multi-tenant architecture too. And microservice communication. The list is long, and rightly so because it shows just how deep the craft is. Everything on that list is a chance to keep building, keep reading and keep breaking things in development so they can be used in production.

Last thing, I wanted to mention. The myapp project that weaves its way through every chapter of this book is pure fiction, but the problems it solves are very real. At the moment, there's probably a developer somewhere who's got an N+1 query that they didn't even know they had. Someone else is watching a scheduled backup fail quietly because of a stale overlap lock. Another is trying to understand why their job queue is growing instead of draining. These are solvable problems, and the people solving them are worth supporting. And don't be afraid to share what you learn. So, get those team members to write up the internal documentation they'd find useful. The idea is to make the code base more readable than you found it. That generosity has a huge impact, which can't really be measured in traditional ways.

It's better to build things that are worth maintaining. So, keep things that are worth building.

Until the next one, thanks for reading!

Thank You

www.ingramcontent.com/pod-product-compliance
Lightning Source LLC
Chambersburg PA
CBHW080215170726
48282CB00030B/1125
* 9 7 8 9 3 4 9 1 7 4 8 2 5 *